UNDERSTANDING
the Art of
Prayer (Revisited)

The most powerful and influential person on earth is a man or woman who knows how to pray effectively, and move the mighty hand that controls all things.

Rev. Dr. Caesar O. Benedo

This book was originally published as part of "Understanding the Art of Prayer."

Copyright © 2015 by Caesar Benedo

All right reserved. No part of this publication may be reproduced, stored in a retrieval system, or transmitted in any form or by any means - electronic, mechanical, photocopying, recording, scanning or otherwise-except for brief quotations in critical reviews or articles, without the prior permission of the copyright holder.

Understanding the Art of Prayer (Revisited)

Copyright © 2017 by Caesar Benedo

ISBN-13: 978-99919-71-90-2

Note: personal pronouns for God, Jesus and the Holy Spirit are lowercased in keeping with the different Bible versions used in this book.

Scripture quotations marked KJV are taken from the Authorized King James version © 1991 by World Bible Publishers, Inc.

Scripture quotations marked NIV are taken from the New International version © 1973, 1978, 1984 by the International Bible Society

Scripture quotations marked NKJV are taken from the New King James version © 1982 by Thomas Nelson, Inc.

Scripture quotations marked NASB are taken from the New America Standard Bible © 1960, 1962, 1963, 1968, 1971, 1972, 1973, 1975, 1977, 1995 by The Lockman Foundation.

Scripture quotations marked NLT are taken from the Holy Bible, New Living Translation ®, copyright © 1996, 2004 by Tyndale Charitable Trust. Used by permission of Tyndale House Publishers. All rights reserved.

Scripture quotations marked ESV are taken from the Holy Bible, English Standard Version Copyright © 2001 by Crossway Bibles, a division of Good News Publishers

Scripture quotations marked AMP are taken from the Amplified Bible © 1954, 1958, 1962, 1964, 1965, 1987 by The Lockman Foundation.

Scripture quotations marked THE MESSAGE are taken from THE MESSAGE: The Bible in Contemporary Language © 2002 by Eugene H. Peterson. All rights reserved.

Scripture quotations marked HCSB are taken from the Holman Christian Standard Bible © 1999, 2000, 2002, 2003 by Holman Bible Publishers, Nashville, Tennessee.

Scripture quotations marked RSV are taken from the Revised Standard Version of the Bible copyright © 1946, 1952, and 1971 the Division of Christian Education of the National Council of the Churches of Christ in the United States of America. Used by permission. All rights reserved.

ACKNOWLEDGEMENT

A special thanks to the following people for their love, support and prayer to make this book a reality. Mr. and Mrs. Ononiwu, Mr. and Mrs. Ugwulor, Mrs. Sheyi Bonou, Pastor Fadel Akpiti, Mr. Samuel Fabrice Yomo, Pastor Samuel Kalu, Mr. and Mrs. Odjo, Mr. Kingsley Eme, Mr. and Mrs. Fajemirokun, Mrs. Vivian Asempapa, Mrs. Georgette Gbesset Baffoh, Pastor Veronica Bampoe-Darko, Pastor Maximo Deleon, Rev. Emenike Paul Ezechiluo, Rev. Lucile Sossou, Prophet Holy Joy, Rev. Dr. Nicaise Laleye, Rev. Alphonse Dagnonnoueton, Rev. and Pastor Mrs. Tigo, Rev. Isidore Godonou, Rev. Mrs. and Bishop Meshack Okonkwo and so on.

A million thanks to the members of my family for your love, encouragement, care, and support. May God richly bless you all.

I want to use this opportunity to express my appreciation to Pastor Benjamin Opeyemi Olaosebikan, and Pastor Eric Osei Yaw for their brotherly support, encouragement, and prayer.

A special thanks to Bishop Kwesi Adutwum for your love, encouragement, advice, support, and prayer. I'm indeed thankful to God for your life and for the incredible support you gave me. May God richly bless you.

A special thanks to Rev. Mrs Betty N. Coleman for your love, encouragement, support and prayer. May God richly bless and reward you for the great work you are doing for the kingdom.

I want to use this opportunity to express my gratitude to Pastor Zina Pierre for your love, support and prayer. May the Lord continue to bless you.

A special thanks to my Bishop, James Nana Ofori Attah for your love, encouragement, support and prayer. May the Lord continue to bless you.

I want to use this opportunity to express my gratitude to Apostle Michael Adeyemi Adefarasin for bringing out the best in me. I admire your commitment to excellence, your sincere desire to make a difference and your love for good work.

A special thanks to my papa, the archbishop Nicholas Duncan-Williams (founder of Action Chapel International), for your prayers, leadership, and spiritual guidance. May God continue to use you to raise and empower men and women to fulfil their divine purpose.

Words cannot convey how much I appreciate the love, care, support and prayer of senior deacon, and mama Georgina Lamptey for all the investment both of you made in my life. Thank you for standing by me at the very moment I needed it the most. May the Lord richly bless you.

DEDICATION

If you are having challenges building active prayer life, or you were once very effective in prayer, but it seems like you have lost the zeal to pray, and to everyone who desires to be more effective and consistent in prayer, but don't know what to do, this is for you.

Table of Contents

ACKNOWLEDGEMENT..III
DEDICATION...V
PRAYER 1
INTRODUCTION 3

Chapter One   FUNDAMENTALS OF PRAYER 7

What is prayer 8
Why we pray 14
How to pray 21

Chapter Two   PRAYER CLOSET 25

Chapter Three   LEVELS OF PRAYER 29

Asking..29
Seeking 30
Knocking 33

Chapter Four   RULES OF ENGAGEMENT 37

Biblical truths 48
Biblical concepts..48
Biblical principles 48

Chapter Five   HINDRANCES TO PRAYER 49

Ignorance 49
Sin 51
Wrong motive 53
God refusing to answer 55
Demonic operation 58
Wrong timing 61
Lack of faith 65

Chapter Six   MECHANISM OF PRAYER 67

Chapter Seven   KEYS TO EFFECTIVE PRAYER 79

Relationship with God 79
Humility 81
Knowledge 83
Praise and worship 84
Passion 87
Fellowship 90
Determination 92
Prayer language 96
Faith 106
Gratitude 108
Sacrifice 111
Fasting 116
Commitment 124

Chapter Eight DYNAMICS OF PRAYER 127

Chapter Nine WONDERS OF PRAYER 135

The prayer of Jabez 135
Nature of Jabez's prayer 140

Chapter Ten THE PRAYER OF CORNELIUS 143

Chapter Eleven PRAYER WORKS 151

Peter miraculous escape from jail 152
Protective and preventive power of prayer 154
Role of prayer in discovering your divine purpose ... 161
Role of prayer in birthing your prophetic destiny 170

IMPORTANT ABBREVIATION 175
PRAYER OF SALVATION 177

PRAYER

Heavenly Father, in agreement with the Scripture that says the entrance of your word gives light and understanding to the simple (Ps.119:130), I beseech you to enlighten the eyes of my heart that I may understand the mystery of prayer as I read this book. Grant me insight and the grace to take hold of the truth, just as you did for Lydia in Acts16:14, when you opened her heart to receive the truth spoken by the apostle Paul about your Son Jesus.

By the power of the Holy Spirit, I pull down every imagination, argument and thought that does not conform to biblical truths, concepts and principles that the wicked may want to use to hinder me from accepting the truth in this book. It is written that I shall know the truth, and the truth will set me free (Jn.8:32).

Dear Lord, open my eyes to the truth in this book and deliver me from the spirit of error in Jesus name. Amen!

The president of the United States does it, the Prime Minister of Israel does it, the Chairman of the Palestinian People does it, and the Queen of England does it. Jews do it, Muslims do it, Hindus do it, Buddhists do it, pagans do it, heathens do it, Christians do it, everyone does it. Few are sure it works, and even less believe it is necessary. What is it? Prayer!

— *Dr. Myles Munroe*

INTRODUCTION

Prayer is not just a religious activity, but a way of life. This is why we learn the art of prayer. In his book, *Prayer - The Art of Believing*, Neville Goddard writes, "Prayer is an art and requires practice." The art of prayer is the skill required for effective and consistent prayer. It is the "how-to" and the "know-how" of prayer. Learning the art of prayer is like learning the art of negotiation, speaking, making friends, and so on. Some call it the discipline of prayer.

The free online dictionary includes in its definition of an "art" the following: a skill that is attained by study, practice, or observation. The art of prayer can be learned through study, practice, and observation. Those who understand the art of prayer master the "how-to" and the "know-how."

This book provides practical guidelines for effective prayer. It explains basic requirements for consistent prayer. It teaches what prayer is, how it works, what it does, how to pray, hindrance to prayer, laws of prayer, levels of prayer, keys to consistent prayer, things that add weight to prayer, types of prayer etc. It addresses some reasons many pray without receiving answers, and what to do about it.

UNDERSTANDING the Art of Prayer (Revisited)

Prayer is one of the most taught subjects in the Christendom because of its importance. However, it is perhaps the most misunderstood. More work has been done on the "need to pray" than on "how to pray." Most of us know we need prayer and we can give many reasons why we have to pray. The major problem Christians are facing today is the proper understanding of the "how-to" of prayer. To produce results through prayer, you have to know the techniques that work.

A lot of people are very reluctant to pray either because they see it as hard work or as a waste of time. Others who were once motivated and very eager to pray became discouraged after praying about a particular thing for a long time without an answer. Some even ask weather prayer really works at all.

Prayer works wonders! It changes life and situation. It moves the mighty hand that controls the heavens and earth. If it is not working for you, it's probably because you are ignoring some vital factors that make it work. God hears and answers prayers. He will continue to do so because he never changes. Prayer has always worked and will continue to work for those who learn the "how-to" and acquire the "know-how."

Understanding the art of prayer is the master key that kick-starts your prayer life and moves it to a new dimension. That is why this book is a must-read for everyone who desires a consistent prayer life. It is the product of my many years of experiences as the prayer warrior leader and head of intercessory group in our church and other prayer networks where I taught many how to pray.

INTRODUCTION

I will be sharing with you some personal insights and experiences I got as the national prayer director of Action Chapel International Benin (ACI) for nine years. I will be sharing with you the things we learned both from our papa, the Archbishop Nicholas Duncan-Williams, who is known worldwide as the apostle of strategic prayer; and from other notable men and women of God who taught us how to pray, amongst whom is Apostle Michael Adeyemi Adafarasin, Bishop Derek Nunekpeku, etc.

I have always heard my papa the archbishop say that God can't do anything for humanity until somebody prays - for it is unscriptural for him to come to the earth to do anything without invitation through prayer because he gave the earth to mankind - and that prayer is the vehicle that moves and carries from eternity into time what God has prepared for us. Heaven does not respond to the earth until prayer goes up. Most importantly, prayer is the meeting place between divinity and humanity. What a mystery!

Please join me and let's explore together this all-important subject: "the art of prayer." I pray that the Holy Spirit will open your eyes of understanding as you read this book, and use the information in it to revive your prayer life. Welcome onboard!

Ask and it will be given to you; seek and you will find; knock and the door will be opened to you. For everyone who asks receives; he who seeks finds; and to him who knocks, the door will be opened. "Which of you, if his son asks for bread, will give him a stone? Or if he asks for a fish, will give him a snake? If you, then, though you are evil, know how to give good gifts to your children, how much more will your Father in heaven give good gifts to those who ask him!

(Matt. 7:7-11 NIV)

CHAPTER 1

FUNDAMENTALS OF PRAYER

The Lord Jesus did so many astounding miracles during his earthly ministry that if every one of them were written, the whole world would not have enough room for the books that would be written (Jn21:25). He healed the sick, raised the dead, casted out devils, opened blind eyes, cured leprosy, turned water to wine, and he multiplied bread and fish for thousands of people to eat. However, the only thing his disciples asked him to teach them how to do, having watched him very closely for about three and a half years was prayer. This establishes the fact that prayer is taught, and whatever is taught can be learned.

Luke 11:1 recounts how the Lord Jesus was praying in a certain place. When he finished, one of his disciples came to him and said, "Lord, teach us to pray just as John taught his disciples." In response to their request, the Lord laid out a pattern for prayer to guide them. According to him, prayer is taught, and there is a pattern for effective prayer that anyone genuinely interested in understanding the art must learn.

UNDERSTANDING the Art of Prayer (Revisited)

First, the disciples observed his way of prayer and noticed that he knew something that they did not know (what you know about prayer determines your attitude).

Second, they learned from John the Baptist that prayer is taught (it can be learned). Whatever is taught can be learned. The fact John taught his disciples how to pray means Jesus could also teach them what he knew about prayer. The desire to learn from others what they already know about the subject puts you in a position to receive information that will enhance your prayer life.

Third, knowledge is power. Knowing what Jesus knew about prayer would change how the disciples prayed. Understanding the "how-to" of prayer will change your attitude toward prayer. One of the main reasons many see prayer as hard work is because they do not have a proper understanding of the subject. Prayer is a broad but very essential subject to Christendom. It must be well taught, learned, and practiced. Those who have proper knowledge and understanding of prayer, do a lot through it. What you know about prayer determines the consistency of your prayer life.

Fourth, they could understand the art of prayer by learning from their master, practicing whatever he taught them, and observing him very closely to learn more techniques and strategies for consistent prayer. Study, practice, and observation are keys to understanding the art of prayer.

WHAT IS PRAYER

My papa, the Archbishop Duncan-Williams, defines prayer as a supernatural weapon that God has made available to you

FUNDAMENTALS OF PRAYER

and me to deploy him and to deploy his angels, and to enforce and superimpose his kingdom and his will over the kingdom of men and over the works of the enemy. According to him, prayer is the vehicle that carries out the purposes of God on Earth. Heaven can't do anything for humanity unless we pray.

In response to the disciples' request for Jesus to teach them how to pray, he said, "When you pray, say":

Father, allowed be your name, your kingdom come. Give us each day our daily bread. Forgive us our sins, for we also forgive everyone who sins against us. And lead us not into temptation.
(Lk. 11:2-4 NIV)

We notice in the above scripture that the only way God's kingdom and purposes can be done on earth is through the vehicle of prayer. The passage also reveals that prayer is both communication and relationship. It begins with an act of worship and places the interest of the kingdom over personal agenda.

Divine will and counsel can only be born through the womb of prayer, and without prayer God cannot manifest on earth. This is because God gave the right of rulership to mankind, but Adam ceded it to Satan through sin. For this reason, Satan is the governor of this world, as he pointed out during the temptation of the Lord Jesus - claiming that the authority and glory of all the kingdoms of the world had been given to him, and that he would give it to whomever he willed, in an attempt to make Jesus worship him (Lk.4:5-6). I will expand on this as we proceed.

Prayer is an expression of faith and dependency on God. These are the fundamentals of prayer that everyone genuinely interested in a consistent prayer life has to know.

UNDERSTANDING the Art of Prayer (Revisited)

We worship God for who he is and praise him for what he does. A life of prayer is one of worship, relationship, communication, faith, holiness, forgiveness, giving, sacrifice, power, authority, and so on.

In my book, *The Origin and Purpose of Prayer*, under the heading, "Understanding the concept of prayer," I explained that prayer is the only means by which humans give spirit beings, whether the living God or demons, the legal right to act on earth; through the authority God conferred on humankind in the beginning when he made us the governor of the earth. For the benefit of those who haven't read the book, below is an excerpt.

"… prayer is the only means by which humans give spirit beings, whether the living God or demons, the legal right to act in the earth realm; through the authority God conferred on humankind in the beginning when he made us the governor of the earth.

Prayer becomes the spiritual bridge that connects the spirit world and the earth. It is the only means by which God's ability to do things connects with the right of man to act on earth to effect changes amongst humans. Prayer is the only weapon that connects the heaven, and the earth. God has the ability (power) to do things, but humankind retains the right (authority) to act on earth. Prayer connects God's power with human's authority to change things in the world.

It came about as a result of the structure and order that God established in the beginning between the heavens, and the earth. The heavens is God's habitation, while the earth is man's territory. The order is that no spirit can act on earth without the cooperation or permission of humans who God put in charge of the earth realm. The Lord retains both the ability to do things and the right to act in heaven.

FUNDAMENTALS OF PRAYER

He doesn't need anyone's approval or permission to work in heaven. But on earth, he needs the invitation or authorization of humans to do things. This is why heaven needs our prayers. Heaven does not respond to the earth until prayer goes up, says my papa the archbishop Nicholas Duncan-Williams.

Anytime there is a call for prayer, know that God is seeking the right to do things amongst humans, and he can only obtain it through the prayer of the church. No spirit being can interfere with earth affairs or act in the earth realm without the prayers of humans that give them the right to do things in the world. This is why prayer cuts across all boundaries, be it religion, language, culture, race, geographical location, social ranks, and so on."

Speaking on the "power of intercession", Dr. Cindy Trimm explains that one of the things you have to do if you want to really persevere in prayer is to discipline yourself. "Learn the fundamentals, and then when you learn the fundamentals, you will begin to have fun. You cannot have fun without fundamentals." To understand the art of prayer, one has to learn the fundamentals of prayer (what prayer is, why we pray, how to pray, when to pray etc.). Prayer becomes exciting when you learn the fundamentals.

The Lord Jesus started his teaching by saying, "When you pray, say:" because prayer engages both the one who prays and whomever he prays to. It is a communication between humans and God.It connects us to God and ushers us into his presence. It is an expression of our faith, trust, and hope in him.Dr. Trimm puts it this way, "Prayer is man's declaration of dependency on God." We pray because we know God exists and that he hears and answers prayers.

UNDERSTANDING the Art of Prayer (Revisited)

There is no better way to express our faith in God than prayer. The essence of prayer is faith, says Goddard.

Prayer is not a mere religious activity but an act of faith that gives humans access to the spiritual world, where power and authority to effect changes on earth is derived. The same way prayer gives humans access to the spiritual world, it also gives God access to the physical world. E. M. Bounds writes, "God shapes the world by prayer. The more prayer there is in the world, the better the world will be, the mightier the forces against evil."

Dr. Myles Munroe, speaking on the "kingdom pattern for prayer," includes in his definition of prayer the following: "Prayer is not a religious activity. Prayer is earthly license for heavenly influence. Prayer is mankind giving God permission to interfere in earth affairs…. Prayer is heaven's power imparting earth through man's earthly authority…. Prayer is mankind giving heaven authority to perform God's word on earth."

This is one of the reasons prayer is so powerful, a treasure in the hand of those who master the art. You must know to whom you address your prayers, because prayer establishes a bond between you and the one to whom you pray.

Prayer begins with knowing who God is and what he means to you, which is the reason why the Lord Jesus asks us to address him as "Our Father." Cultivating a consistent prayer life starts with knowing who God is, what he does, why you need him, where he is, how he works, what his plans are, and accepting him as your father. Prayer involves a connection, communion, and communication. It is an expression of faith in God.

FUNDAMENTALS OF PRAYER

Prayer is a spiritual exercise that moves the mighty hand that controls all things. It is the master key that opens the heavens and changes the course of things. It can determine the outcome of any event. James 5:17-18 tells how the prophet Elijah used prayer to close the heavens over the land of Israel for three and a half years so that it would not rain because of their sins and iniquities. Again he prayed, and the heavens gave rains.

In Luke 3:21-22, the Lord Jesus used the same prayer to open the heavens over his ministry, to provoke the release of the Holy Spirit in bodily form on him; and to cause a voice to proceed from the Father to validate his earthly ministry (this is what prayer can do).

Prayer is not just a gift but a lifestyle. That is why we learn the discipline of prayer. Those who are very prayerful would tell you how much it changed their lives because of the rules of engagement. Prayer establishes lines and boundaries as to how you live, where you go, who your friends are, how you dress, what you say, read, watch, etc. It brings you to the place of sacrifice and separates you from things that do not please God.

Since prayer is a spiritual discipline, it favors things that gratifies the Spirit and opposes the lusts and desires of the flesh, for the works of the flesh put men in enmity against God (Rom.8:5-11, Gal.5:17-25). Honest men and women of prayer walk in holiness because prayer sanctifies them, it creates the atmosphere that enhances holy living, and it opens their eyes to revelation knowledge.

WHY WE PRAY

When God made mankind to rule over all the things he created on earth, and gave him the legal right to govern the world, he did not include himself in the dominion mandate that he gave humanity (Gen.1:26-28). For this reason, it is unscriptural for God to come to the earth to do anything among men without the invitation or cooperation of mankind. Whatever God gives, he won't take back, according to Romans 11:29.

As long as the seeds of Adam live on earth, the world remains their domain, but the right to govern it was ceded to Satan in the Garden of Eden through deception and manipulation. As a result, Satan holds the earth on lease until Christ's Millennium reign when Satan will be bound for a thousand years to stop him from exercising authority over the world (Rev.20:1-3). However, Satan will be set free for a short time after the thousand years is over to continue his reign and deception of humanity until he is finally judged and thrown into the lake of fire (verses 7-10).

Since God made the earth man's jurisdiction, and Satan deceitfully stole the right of rulership from humans, the Lord cannot interfere with earth affairs unless humans pray. Otherwise, he would violate his word and principle. Matthew 6:8 declares that God knows what we need before we ask, and verse 9 teaches us the pattern for prayer and encourages us to pray.

My question is, if God knows what we need before we ever pray, why should he ask us to pray? Can't he just give us that which we need without us asking for it? Isn't he the creator of heaven and earth, the possessor of all things? Why must we pray for things before he grants them? Why should we pray for his kingdom to come and for his will to be done on earth as it is in heaven?

FUNDAMENTALS OF PRAYER

The answers to all of the above questions is that God created the earth, gave it to man, gave him free will and excluded himself in the management of human affairs. He would not interfere or implement his agenda within man's domain unless mankind invites him, and the only way to invite him is prayer.

I came across a passage in the Bible that amazes me whenever I read it. The Lord said in Revelation 3:20 that he stands at the door and knocks. If anyone hears his voice and opens the door, he will come in and eat with the person. Why would God seek human permission and consent before doing anything in our domain? I believe the reason is because he gave mankind free will and will not violate our boundaries. Prayer gives him the judicial right to come to human territory. For this reason, he gave us a pattern for prayer, to teach us both how to pray and what to pray about.

Dr. Myles says the first and most important principle of earthly influence is prayer. I believe the reason for this is because prayer opens the heavens, gives God access to the earth, births his kingdom, and superimposes his will over the kingdoms of men and over the works of the wicked. No one is more influential on earth than a person who knows how to effectively pray. He can bring God on the scene, initiate change and determine the course of things by prayer.

In Luke 22:40 and 46, the Bible asks us to pray that we may not enter into temptation. The power to avert evil is released through prayer. It raises the spiritual antennae and builds a hedge of protection around those who are consistent in the art, making them less vulnerable to the manipulation of the wicked. Prayer is a strong weapon!

UNDERSTANDING the Art of Prayer (Revisited)

We live in a world that is ruled by the devil (Jn.12:31, 14:30, 16:11). 1 John 5:19b says that the whole world lies under the control of the evil one. Micah 2:1-2 talks about those who devise iniquity and work out evil on their beds. When morning light comes, they carry out their wicked plans because it is in their power to do so. They harass people and take their properties by force. This is so because Satan and his cohorts reign in this world.

Since the only one who has the legal right to act on earth is human (a spirit-being with body), and that mankind ceded the authority to Satan through deception, God sent his Word (Jesus of Nazareth, the Son of the living God) to die for the sins of humanity; and restore our lost authority, which the devil stole (Phil.2:5-11, Heb.2:9-14, 1 Jn. 3:8). Having disarmed the powers and authorities, he openly disgraced them and he restored the dominion to mankind. He inaugurated a new era of God's kingdom on earth and established the church – his body as his agency on earth – before ascending bodily to represent humanity in the courtroom of heaven.

God uses the prayer of the church to birth his agenda and establish his will on earth. He does nothing on earth without the prayer of Saints. Churches move his hand through prayer to work among humans. God won't bypass the authority he gave mankind over the earth, and neither will he interfere with human affairs unless someone invites him. We pray to give heaven access and permission to act in this world that lies in wickedness. This is why the Bible says we must pray — so that we can give God access to earth through the authority he gave us and he would not violate that, says Dr. Myles.

FUNDAMENTALS OF PRAYER

In Jesus' pattern for prayer, he asked us to pray for God's kingdom to come and that his will be done on earth as it is in heaven (Matt.6:10). The reign of God and his will cannot be established in this world unless humans birth it through prayer. God will stop acting when humans stop praying. The only thing that allows him to work on earth is the prayers of the Saints. No prayer, no license.

During Jesus earthly ministry, when everybody came to the Jordan to be baptized by John, Jesus knew that for him to experience what other people didn't experience, he had to do what others didn't do. The Bible says he prayed after his baptism and opened the heavens. His prayer also caused the Holy Spirit to descend on him in bodily form like a dove and a voice to come from heaven to validate his ministry. As the Son of Man living on earth, the only way the Father and the Holy Spirit could interfere in his affair was through prayer, because he was in man's domain. God honors his principles; he won't violate his word for any reason.

A lot of people think we pray because of our needs, but scripture says the opposite. In his teaching on prayer, the Lord Jesus places the need of the kingdom above ours. He admonishes us to pray first for God's kingdom to come and for his will to be done on earth as it is in heaven before asking him to meet our needs.

Prayer is one of the primary means by which the kingdom of heaven invades the earth. It enhances the birth of God's reign and creates the platform on which his will is established. Without prayer, the kingdom of heaven cannot do much on earth. Heaven stops working on earth when humans stop praying.

UNDERSTANDING the Art of Prayer (Revisited)

The main reason prayer brings solutions to human problems and changes lives is because when divinity meets humanity, something miraculous happens. Prayer causes heaven to impart on the earth. Through it, God's power is released to change things. The more we pray, the more power we activate and release from heaven.

The apostle James says that if anyone among you is afflicted, troubled, suffering, or in hardship, let him pray. If anyone is happy, cheerful, or merry, let him sing praise. If anyone is sick, let him call on the elders of the church to pray and anoint him with oil in the name of the Lord. For the prayer offered in faith will heal the sick, and the Lord will make him well.

Is any one of you in trouble? He should pray. Is anyone happy? Let him sing songs of praise. Is any one of you sick? He should call the elders of the church to pray over him and anoint him with oil in the name of the Lord. And the prayer offered in faith will make the sick person well; the Lord will raise him up. If he has sinned, he will be forgiven. Therefore confess your sins to each other and pray for each other so that you may be healed. The prayer of a righteous man is powerful and effective.
(Jas. 5:13-16NIV)

We see in this passage that prayer is the antidote for affliction, trouble, hardship, suffering, and sickness, from God's point of view. Otherwise, he would have recommended other courses of action for these kinds of situations. For him to point out through the mouth of his apostle that we should pray when afflicted and praise when cheerful means that prayer provokes the miraculous.

FUNDAMENTALS OF PRAYER

When Job was afflicted, he maintained his integrity, disputed with his friends, argued his case, cursed the day he was born, longed to see God face to face, etc. He did everything else but pray. God had to get a way to make him pray by sending his three friends to him for prayer. Job 42:10 declares that the Lord restored Job's fortune when he had prayed for his friends. Though prayer was the solution to his affliction, Job did not pray until God asked him to.

Another good example is the prophet Jonah whom God sent to the great city of Nineveh to preach against it. Instead of obeying God's command, Jonah bought a ticket for a ship going to Tarshish and went on board in an attempt to escape from the Lord. For this reason, God sent a great wind to the sea that threatened to break the ship apart. Everyone in the ship was so afraid that each one cried out to their respective god, but Jonah went down below deck, lay and fell deeply asleep. When the captain saw him, he said, "How can you sleep? Get up and call on your God! Maybe he will take notice of us, and we will not perish."

Finally they decided to cast lots to find out who is responsible for the calamity, and the lots fell on Jonah. When they asked him what they should do to calm the sea, he asked them to throw him into the sea. Chapter1:14 says that the people prayed to God to forgive their action as they threw Jonah into the raging sea, but the man of God did not pray until he had spent three days and night in the belly of the fish God sent to swallow him up. While in the belly of the fish, Jonah cried out to God in prayer and the Lord commanded the fish to vomit him to dry land.

UNDERSTANDING the Art of Prayer (Revisited)

The solution to Jonah's trouble, hardship, and affliction was prayer. However, that was the one thing he refused to do until he found himself in the belly of the fish for three days and nights (Jon.1:1-17, 2:1-10). Don't wait until things fall apart before you pray. It is true that prayer brings healing, deliverance and restoration; it also has the ability to prevent misfortune.

From the time Christ inaugurated a new era of God's kingdom on earth until now, there has been a continuous battle between the kingdom of light and darkness, with both striving to control the earth. One of the reasons the Lord Jesus asked us to pray to birth God's kingdom and will on earth is that it causes the kingdom of heaven to invade and take full control of the earth. Prayer gives the believers advantage over the wicked because it moves the hand of God and causes him to act on earth (ushers in his reign and establishes his will).

One of the things the Bible repeatedly asks us to do is pray without ceasing (Lk.18:1, Eph.6:18, Col.1:3, 9, 4:2-3, 12, 1 Thes.5:17, 2 Thes.1:11, 1 Tim.2:8). I believe the reason for this is because prayer advances the interest of the kingdom of heaven on earth and changes human lives. Nothing gives heaven the legal right to act in this world but prayer. Divinity meets humanity in the place of prayer. It births God's kingdom on earth and superimposes his will over the works of mankind. When heaven reigns, humans live in harmony, and for heaven to reign on earth, it takes prayer.

I encourage you from today forward to pray with meaning. Do it with the understanding that prayer is not just a religious activity but an art of faith that allows heaven to impart the earth and change human lives and circumstances.

FUNDAMENTALS OF PRAYER

No matter what situation you are in, you can change it. Prayer provokes divine intervention, and when God steps into your situation, he changes all that concerns you.

HOW TO PRAY

I mentioned earlier, how the Lord Jesus was praying in a certain place. When he finished, one of his disciples came and asked him to teach them how to pray. In response, he said, "When you pray, say…"

First, the disciples knew the Lord Jesus understands some prayer techniques and strategies. Second, they knew from John the Baptist's experience that prayer is taught. Third, they knew it is possible to learn how to pray. Fourth, for the Lord Jesus to say, "When you pray, say…" means that prayer begins with saying something, and what you say in prayer is very important. You can only talk about what you know. What you know about prayer determines what you say when you pray. To pray effectively, you have to learn how to pray.

The Bible declares in Romans 8:26 that we do not know what we should pray for as we ought, while James 4:3 says the reason we don't receive answers for our prayers is because we ask with wrong motives. It is one thing to pray, it is another to receive what you ask for in prayer. The reason many don't produce positive results in prayer is because they lack basic knowledge about how to pray. Learning how to pray is essential to building a consistent prayer life. To effectively pray, one must understand the different dynamics involved.

UNDERSTANDING the Art of Prayer (Revisited)

Prayer is broad and profound. It requires continuous studies and practice. To master the art, you must make some sacrifices.

In order to learn how to pray, you have got to pray, says Dr. Trimm. The Lord's model for prayer begins with, "When you pray, say:" Learning "what" to say and "how" to say it matters a lot in prayer. Matthew 6:7 warns against using vain repetition in prayer, adding that one is not heard because of many words. Verse 8 says God knows exactly what we need before we ask him.

The truth is that everyone who prays desires to be heard and answered regardless of how it is done. No one ever wants to spend their time in prayer without results. In the same vein, God wants to answer all prayers and grant all desires. He wouldn't ask us to pray if he wasn't going to answer.

From the little we have learned so far, there is no doubt that God needs our prayer to work on earth. Having said that, let's not forget God works in accordance with his words and the principles he established. He won't approve whatever does not agree with his will and counsel (Eph.1:11). Everything must pass the litmus test of his will to gain approval. This is why knowing the will of God for every situation is very important.

The Bible declares in Romans 12:2 that we shouldn't conform to the world but have our minds renewed so that we can discern the will of God – i.e. what is good, pleasing, and perfect in his sight.

The Lord Jesus spoke a parable in Luke 18:9-14 about two men who went up to the temple to pray, one a Pharisee and the other a tax collector. He explained how the tax collector went home justified rather than the Pharisee because of his attitude.

FUNDAMENTALS OF PRAYER

Some people spend a lot of time praying about a particular issue and wonder why they don't receive answers. It is not the amount of time you spend praying that determines the result you produce. There are many things that add value to prayer (we will look at the different factors as we proceed).

James 5:17-18 says the prophet Elijah was a man like us, and he prayed earnestly that it might not rain, and for three years and six months it did not rain on the earth. Scripture beautifully points out the primary reason his prayer produced such an outstanding result was that he prayed earnestly. The prophet could close or open the heavens at any time because he learned to pray fervently. Verse 16c says the fervent prayer of a righteous man avails much.

We can produce the same result Elijah did in his time by learning how to pray fervently. Men of old did wonders through prayers. God hasn't changed! He is the same yesterday, today, and forever (Heb.13:8). For us to do wonders through prayer, we must understand the different factors that make prayer work.

"And when you pray, do not be like the hypocrites, for they love to pray standing in the synagogues and on the street corners to be seen by others. Truly I tell you, they have received their reward in full. 6 But when you pray, go into your room, close the door and pray to your Father, who is unseen. Then your Father, who sees what is done in secret, will reward you.

(Matt. 6:5-6 ESV)

CHAPTER 2

PRAYER CLOSET

My papa, the Archbishop Duncan-Williams, emphatically points out that the secret place of God is the place of prayer. To him, it is the place where divinity meets humanity.

The prayer closet is a place where humans encounter divinity. It is all about you taking time off or withdrawing from your busy schedule or daily routine to be alone with God. There could never be a prayer closet without a personal devotion, because the later establishes the first. It has nothing to do with you setting up a place or raising an altar somewhere. It is a place you turn to give God an undivided attention through prayer, meditation, Bible study, worship or praise. When you spend quality time with God, he takes care of your business.

When the people of the land come before the Lord at the appointed feasts, he who enters by the north gate to worship shall go out by the south gate, and he who enters by the south gate shall go out by the north gate:

UNDERSTANDING the Art of Prayer (Revisited)

no one shall return by way of the gate by which he entered, but each shall go out straight ahead.
(Ezek. 46:9-10ESV)

The Bible says in Matthew 6:6 that when you pray, go into your room and shut the door, pray to your father who is in the secret place, and your father who sees in the secret will reward you openly. In Psalm 91:1, the Bible declares that he who dwells in the secret place of the most high shall abide under the shadow of the almighty. To enjoy the continuous covering of the Lord, we must remain in his secret place, and one of the secret places of God is the prayer closet – where humans encounter divinity.

The Prayer Closet is a place you go to have quality time with the Lord. It is the place where God's agenda for humanity is carried from eternity to time. The power and authority to birth God's kingdom and superimpose his will over the kingdom of men and the works of the wicked is activated in the place of prayer. None is so powerful and influential on earth than the person who dwells in the prayer closet, and control things from a higher dimension. When you spend time in the presence of God, his glory and power rubs off on you.

Exodus 19:10-23 describes how Moses brought the people out of the camp to the foot of the mountain for an encounter with God. Moses had to consecrate them for three days before leading them out as God instructed him. There were rules laid down for them, and any act of violation was punishable by death. The rules of engagement outline the "dos and don'ts". They also define the parameters and establish the lines and boundaries as to what could give you the upper hand or disadvantage you in the place of prayer. They highlight the core values that add weight to prayer.

PRAYER CLOSET

The Lord said to Moses, "Go to the people and consecrate them today and tomorrow, and let them wash their garments and be ready for the third day. For on the third day the Lord will come down on Mount Sinai in the sight of all the people. And you shall set limits for the people all around, saying, 'Take care not to go up into the mountain or touch the edge of it. Whoever touches the mountain shall be put to death. No hand shall touch him, but he shall be stoned or shot; whether beast or man, he shall not live.' When the trumpet sounds a long blast, they shall come up to the mountain." So Moses went down from the mountain to the people and consecrated the people; and they washed their garments. And he said to the people, "Be ready for the third day; do not go near a woman." On the morning of the third day there were thunders and lightnings and a thick cloud on the mountain and a very loud trumpet blast, so that all the people in the camp trembled. Then Moses brought the people out of the camp to meet God, and they took their stand at the foot of the mountain. Now Mount Sinai was wrapped in smoke because the Lord had descended on it in fire. The smoke of it went up like the smoke of a kiln, and the whole mountain trembled greatly. And as the sound of the trumpet grew louder and louder, Moses spoke, and God answered him in thunder. The Lord came down on Mount Sinai, to the top of the mountain. And the Lord called Moses to the top of the mountain, and Moses went up.
(Ex.19:10-20 ESV)

The above passage shows how God instructed the people to wash their clothes and be ready on the third day for an encounter with him. They were not to touch the mountain, and whoever violated the rules was to be stoned or shot with an arrow. In addition, they were not to come near their spouse (sexual purity).

UNDERSTANDING the Art of Prayer (Revisited)

When you know the laws and principles of prayer, and you live by them, it gives you advantage in prayer.

The place of prayer is a refuge and fortress where all kinds of spiritual weapons, whether defensive or offensive, are deployed. It is a command center that controls all spiritual operations. The prayer closet is full of power and authority that is made available to those who make it their dwelling. That is why a person who prays earnestly and spends a lot of time in prayer has so much spiritual authority. Psalm 91:1 talks about the one who dwells or take residence in the secret place of God, which my papa calls the place of prayer.

Exodus 34:28-33 relates how Moses stayed with the Lord forty days and nights on Mount Sinai without food or water to receive the Ten Commandments. When he came down from the mountain, he didn't know that his face was radiant, for the glory of God overshadowed and transformed him while he talked with the Lord.

To attain this dimension, he first came out of the camp, separated himself from the people, climbed to the mountain top, abstained from basic desires of the flesh, tarried in God's presence, and talked with him until his face shone and reflected the glory of God. Those in the camp saw his face shining and were scared to go near him.

Moses had great power and authority because he abided in God's presence forty days and night without food or water. Spending time in prayer can change your life and cause you to reflect the glory of God. The place of prayer is one of glory, blessings, authority, and discipline.

CHAPTER 3

LEVELS OF PRAYER

In Matthew 7:7-8, the Lord says ask, and it will be given to you; seek, and you will find; knock, and it will be opened to you. For everyone who asks receives; the one who seek finds; and to the one who knocks, it will be opened. These are three different levels of prayer. Asking is the first level of prayer that some call the "preliminary level." Seeking is persistent prayer, while knocking is travailing or agonizing prayer.

ASKING

There are levels of prayer, and asking is the first. It is called the "preliminary level" because everyone learning about prayer always thinks it is all about asking and receiving. As they learn more about the subject, however, they realize that prayer goes beyond just asking and receiving.

Prayer is a strong weapon given to humans for effecting changes on earth. People with little knowledge about the art of prayer always focus on themselves when praying.

This is why we learn the fundamentals of prayer. What you know about prayer determines your attitude and what you say in prayer.

The preliminary level is not merely for new converts, as some think, but for all who don't really understand the art of prayer, regardless of how many years they have been in Christ. The passage in Matthew 7:9-11 talks about God giving good gifts to those who ask him. Although the three levels of prayer are centered on asking, the difference is in the "how" and "what" (seek and you will find; knock and the door will open).

James says if anyone lacks wisdom, he should ask God who gives generously without finding fault and it will be given him. But he must ask in faith without doubting, for the one who doubt is like a wave of the sea blown and tossed by the wind. Such person should not expect to receive anything from the Lord, because he is double-minded (Jas.1:5-8). This means that for us to receive what we ask from the Lord, we must ask by faith, and without faith, it is impossible to please God (Heb.11:6).

Faith comes by hearing the word of God (Rom.10:17). When we learn about prayer, the knowledge we receive produces the level of faith we need to obtain things from God. To be effective in this level, we must learn the fundamentals of prayer.

SEEKING

To seek means to search for, look for, pursue, etc. I call this level the "persistent prayer." It is all about knowing what you really want and keeping at it in prayer until you get it.

LEVELS OF PRAYER

The Lord Jesus tells a parable in Luke 18:1-8 that illustrates the importance of persistent prayer. The story is about a widow who repeatedly went to a certain judge for justice against her adversary. The judge, who neither feared God nor cared about people, ignored her for a while. But he finally said to himself, "Even though I don't fear God or care what people think, because this widow keeps bothering me, I will see that she gets justice so that she won't wear me out by her continual coming."

The unjust judge granted the widow her desire because she kept worrying him about it and wouldn't let him have his peace. Verse 7 says God won't keep putting off his elect who cry to him day and night, while verse 8 declares he will grant justice to them quickly. The widow got what she was seeking because she persisted. Persistent prayer causes you to break forth.

The apostle Paul explains in 2 Corinthians 12:7-9 how he was given a thorn in the flesh, a messenger of Satan, to torment him in order to keep him from becoming proud because of the great revelations he received from God. For this reason, he pleaded with the Lord to take it away from him. But the Lord said to Paul that his grace was sufficient for him, for his power is made perfect in weakness.

The apostle knew what he wanted, and he pleaded with God three times to take it away. Persistency in prayer produces results if what you are seeking is God's will. That is why knowledge is so essential. The knowledge you have about God's will and the things that make this level of prayer work determine how effective your prayer will be.

UNDERSTANDING the Art of Prayer (Revisited)

To move to the next level, you have to understand the fundamentals, mechanisms, and the basics of effective prayer.

The Bible talks about how the prophet Daniel prayed and God responded to his prayer from the very moment he prayed by sending him an angel. But the prince of the Persian kingdom resisted the angel and detained him twenty-one days. This delayed the answer God gave to Daniel's prayer. Daniel kept at it and persistently sought God through prayer until angel Michael was sent from heaven to release the angel carrying the answer to his prayer from demonic detention. Had Daniel not persisted in prayer, he would not have provoked heavenly reinforcement that lead to the rescue of the angel holding the answer to his prayer from the custody of the prince of the Persian kingdom (Daniel 10:1-13).

The prophet Daniel turned to God and pleaded with him in prayer and fasting. God heard his prayer and granted his request the first day, but Daniel could not receive what the Lord sent him because the demonic principality ruling over the region in which he was living blocked the miracle from landing by capturing the angel carrying it from getting to where Daniel was. Had Daniel only prayed and stopped, he would never have broken through. But he kept at it and pushed until he broke out, broke through, and broke forth.

Cornelius, the Roman military officer, is another man who changed his life through persistent prayer. The passage in Acts 10:1-48 explains how he prayed continually to God until an angel was sent from heaven to tell him that his prayers and alms had come up as a memorial before God.

LEVELS OF PRAYER

He kept at it until his prayer made God change his original plan about the ministry of the word to the gentiles. Paul was the apostle predestined by God to minster the gospel message to the gentiles, while Peter was to reach out to the Jews. At that time, Paul wasn't ready, so God had to use Peter for the occasion.

Cornelius' persistent prayer provoked a divine intervention and direction that changed his life for good, lead him to where Peter was staying, pulled down the stronghold in his mind, overturned the law that was against him, and brought salvation to his home (I'll expand on the prayer of Cornelius in chapter four). Had he not persisted in prayer, God would not have done all he did just to save him and his family.

KNOCKING

This is what I call agonizing, travailing or prevailing prayer. It is a strategic prayer that opens all kinds of doors, whether spiritual or physical. A door is the point of entry and exit — it determines what comes in and goes out of a place.

Travailing prayer is a gateway prayer that allows you to enter the courtroom of heaven and gives you access to the judicial decisions and the executive order of God concerning humanity so that you can birth it in the earth. Nothing leaves heaven and comes to earth until heaven's door opens. This prayer knocks the heavenly door open and causes divine release. Those who operate in this level understand the wonders of prayer, dynamics of prayer, ministry of intercession, art of spiritual warfare, and groaning in the spirit.

UNDERSTANDING the Art of Prayer (Revisited)

Most dictionaries define agony and travail as anguish, extreme pain, distress, grief, sorrow, misery, labor, hard work, and so on. A person agonizes over an issue that causes extreme pain, discomfort, sorrow, anguish, distress, misery, etc. whether mentally or physically. The pain releases an irresistible burden that makes one cry and wail in prayer.

Hebrews 5:7 reveals how the Lord Jesus offered up prayers and supplications during his days on earth with loud cries and tears to him who was able to save him from death, and he was heard. To rescue humanity from sin and death, he suffered intense pain on the cross and cried out in a loud voice, "My God, my God, why have you forsaken me?" The Father turned his face away from him because he carried the sins of the world to save human souls from eternal damnation (Matt.27:46-50).

When a woman is giving birth, she suffers labor pains (Jn.16:21). Likewise, agonizing prayer causes you to travail like a woman in labor, and when you agonize in prayer, you break out, break through, and break forth both in spirit and physical.

The hallmark of travailing prayer is birthing, because it opens the heavens and causes a divine release. No matter what you have been impregnated with in the spirit, you can deliver it through travailing prayer. The prophet Isaiah said that as soon as Zion travails, she will be brought forth (Is.66:7). When you travail in prayer, it opens the womb of your spirit and causes you to give birth.

Revelation 12:1-6 gives us a picture of a pregnant woman in labor pain getting ready to bring forth. She travails by reason of the pain, and gives birth to a male child who will rule the nation with an iron scepter.

LEVELS OF PRAYER

In the same way a pregnant woman in childbirth gets help from midwives, the Holy Spirit helps us in our weakness when we arrive at this level of prayer by interceding for us with groans that words cannot express (Rom.8:26). When you travail or agonize in prayer, you produce the miraculous. I'll expand on this level of prayer as we continue.

The Bible declares in James 5:17-18 that the prophet Elijah was a human being like we are. He prayed earnestly that it would not rain and it did not rain on the land for three and a half years. 1 Kings 18:41-44 describes how he did it, what it cost him, and the pain he went through to enforce God's word and birth the prophecy through prayer.

The passage says he bent down to the ground and put his face between his knees, after which he sent his servant to go look toward the sea for a sign of the heavy rain that was about to fall. The servant went at first and saw nothing. Elijah sent him back to look whether he would see something until the seventh time, when he saw a cloud as small as a man's hand rising from the sea. Though it took long, the prophet Elijah got what he was seeking because he travailed in prayer.

Some call what he did in this passage the seven dimensions of prayer. That is to say, apart from the three levels of prayer, there are dimensions. This is why everybody does not produce the same result in prayer. People can be on the same level but not the same dimension (I'll expand on this as we proceed).

Matthew 26:37-44 describes how the Lord Jesus became so sorrowful and troubled that he asked his disciples to keep watch with him as he prayed.

UNDERSTANDING the Art of Prayer (Revisited)

The passage shows how he prayed about a particular thing three times because of the struggle between his will and the will of the Father.

Luke's version of this passage says that an angel came from heaven to strengthen him as soon as he prayed for the will of the Father to be done. And being in agony, he prayed earnestly until his sweat became like drops of blood falling to the ground (Lk.22:41-44).

From the two passages, we notice that the Lord Jesus went from persistently seeking to establish his personal will, which was contrary to the original plan of the Father, to superimposing the will of the Father and birthing his prophetic destiny. When he said, "Not my will, but yours be done", he superimposed the Father's will over his own will and released his prophetic destiny.

To do this, scripture says he was in agony, and he prayed more intensely until his sweat fell to the ground like drops of blood. This also establishes the fact that there are dimensions of prayer. He prayed until his sweat became as thick as drops of blood.

CHAPTER 4

RULES OF ENGAGEMENT

There are things people say and do in prayer that are not lawful according to divine order and principles. Understanding the spiritual legal system and how it works is very important in prayer. It is good to understand how the courtroom of heaven functions, and the basis for enforcing judicial decisions and executive order of the Godhead for humanity, nations, community, families, or individual on earth (human territory).

The Godhead is the judge in the courtroom of heaven, and Jesus is our defense attorney who vigorously defends us whenever the devil comes to prosecute and file legal charges against us. The Holy Spirit helps our weakness by giving us the ability to exercise our divine authority and use the heavenly language to present our case in accordance with the will of the Father.

Revelation 12:7-9 recounts how the angel Michael (defense minister of heaven) and his angels fought against the dragon (Satan) when he rebelled against God.

UNDERSTANDING the Art of Prayer (Revisited)

The dragon and his angels fought back, but he was not strong enough to withstand Michael and his angels. The great dragon (ancient serpent, devil, or Satan) lost his place in heaven and was thrown to the earth with his angels.

God didn't fight Satan, because it was not appropriate for him to fight his creature, and neither did he take from the devil all the talents he gave him (he doesn't take back what he gives). Michael fought, resisted, and chased the devil out of heaven.

When Moses died, Satan fought for his body, and when angel Michael intervened to stop the devil from taking the body, scripture says he did not dare to use slanderous words against him (Jude 9). When the first battle took place in heaven, Michael used all means to fight and stopped the devil because heaven is his jurisdiction, but when the battle ground moved to earth, Michael could not use bad words against the devil because he was outside his jurisdiction.

The earth is man's jurisdiction, but Adam ceded it to Satan through sin. This made Satan the governor and god of the world. It is illegal for Michael to fight Satan on earth because it is outside his jurisdiction. He had to refer the case to a higher authority by rebuking him in the name of the Lord since he had no personal legal right to deal with Satan on earth. Knowing what is legally acceptable according to divine judicial system gives you advantage in prayer.

When Michael noticed he had no advantage over the devil because of the location of the battle ground, he changed strategy and referred the case to the Lord, whose jurisdiction has no boundary.

RULES OF ENGAGEMENT

Had he tried to use his personal authority, he would probably have ended up like the angel in Daniel 10:13 who was resisted and detained twenty-one days by the prince of Persia until Michael came to help him.

People command and bind things that they don't have judicial authority to do. Some even command the Father, Son, and Holy Spirit in prayer. To effectively pray, you must know what is lawful according to the scripture. You don't command the one who gives you power and authority.

In Genesis 32:24-26, the Bible narrates how Jacob sent messengers to his brother Esau, who was living in the region of Seir in the land of Edom, so that he might obtain favor and forgiveness from him; for Jacob had stolen Esau's blessing before he fled to Paddan Aram to the house of his mother's father Bethuel.

When his mother Rebekah heard that Esau was planning to kill Jacob, she asked him (Jacob) to flee to her brother Laban in Haran and remain there with him until his brother's anger subsided and he forgot what Jacob did to him (Gen.27:42-45). Jacob stayed with Laban until God commanded him to go back to the land of his fathers (Gen. 31:3).

After twenty years with Laban, Jacob decided to go back home. On the way, he sent messengers and gifts ahead of him to Esau to appease his fury because he was afraid of him. Jacob gave the following instruction to the messengers he sent, "Your servant Jacob says, 'I have been staying with Laban and have remained there till now. I have cattle and donkeys, sheep and goats, menservants and maidservants. Now I am sending this message to my lord that I may find favor in your eyes.'"

UNDERSTANDING the Art of Prayer (Revisited)

When the messengers returned to Jacob, they said, "We went to your brother Esau, and now he is coming to meet you, and four hundred men are with him." For this reason, Jacob divided his household, along with the flocks, herds, and camels into two groups because he was greatly afraid and in distress. He thought if his brother Esau attacked one group, the other group might escape. Having done that, he prayed:

God of my father Abraham and God of my father Isaac, the Lord, who said to me, "Go back to your land and to your family, and I will cause you to prosper," I am unworthy of all the kindness and faithfulness You have shown Your servant. Indeed, I crossed over this Jordan with my staff, and now I have become two camps. Please rescue me from the hand of my brother Esau, for I am afraid of him; otherwise, he may come and attack me, the mothers, and their children. You have said, "I will cause you to prosper, and I will make your offspring like the sand of the sea, which cannot be counted."
(Gen. 32:9-12 HCSB)

After the prayer, Jacob selected a gift from his possession to present to his brother Esau, so that he might use it to appease him for stealing his birthright and blessing. He also sent all he had ahead and he remained alone in the camp. Suddenly, a man visited him and wrestled with him till daybreak. When he realized that he could not prevail against Jacob, he touched his hip and put it out of joint.

Remember, Jacob had an issue with his brother for stealing his blessing and when he heard Esau was coming to him with four hundred men, fear gripped him, so he prayed for God to deliver him from his brother's hand. God had instructed him to return to his father's house and possess the land he promised to his father Abraham.

RULES OF ENGAGEMENT

But Jacob had taken it through deception, by pretending to be Esau when Isaac prayed for him.

The Lord needed to fix all of that before Jacob reached home. So he visited Jacob while he was alone, because Jacob could not face his brother Esau and possess the land the way he was. Some things needed to be corrected before he could possess the blessing. I believe God didn't go to Jacob to engage in a fight but to help him because Jacob had prayed for his intervention. Perhaps Jacob initiated the fight to defend himself when he noticed a stranger in his tent.

When God realized he could not overpower Jacob, he hit his hip and put it out of joint to gain advantage over him. At daybreak, God asked Jacob to let him go but he refused and said, "I will not let you go unless you bless me." Jacob gave him a condition and caused God to agree to his terms before letting him go.

We notice here that though God is all-powerful, he couldn't defeat Jacob – a mortal man — because the battle took place within man's jurisdiction. This gave Jacob advantage on the battlefield to withstand the Lord. For scripture to say God couldn't prevail against him means that Jacob won the fight.

When Jacob asked God for a blessing, he responded by asking him his name. "What is your name?" the man asked. "Jacob," he replied. God could have asked him some other questions before blessing him. Don't forget that this was the same question his father Isaac asked him before blessing him.

When his father Isaac asked about his name, he told him he was Esau and stole his brother's blessing.

Spiritually, the blessing was released on the name Esau not Jacob, even though Jacob had it physically (Isaac confirmed it on the name Esau not Jacob). Two persons had equal right to the blessing, Esau in the spirit and Jacob in the physical.

This was an error that needed to be corrected before Jacob could fully enjoy the blessings of Abraham and escape his brother's fury. "Your name shall no longer be Jacob, but Israel, for you have fought with God and with men, and have won," the man said to him.

Some people only receive their blessings physically, while other personalities or entities control the same blessings spiritually. Since the spiritual world controls the physical, the one who owns it physically do not fully enjoy the blessings because two or more forces are contending for the same blessing. It is one thing to own a thing physically, another is to also own it spiritually. In the physical, the blessings of Abraham was in Jacob's hand. But in the spirit, it belongs to Esau by the decrees and declaration of their father Isaac.

I believe God came to Jacob to correct the error and to change his name so that he could enter the blessing of Abraham the right way, but Jacob took him for an enemy that had come to engage him in battle. So he took his stand to defend himself against the aggression. Though God is almighty, he could not defeat Jacob, because the battle took place within man's domain.

When his brother Esau finally met him, he saw a different man (Israel) and not Jacob, because his identity had changed. God moved the blessing from Jacob and Esau, and confirmed it on Israel. So he ran to meet him and embraced him; he threw his arms around his neck and kissed him. The blessing they were fighting for has now moved from Esau and Jacob to Israel.

RULES OF ENGAGEMENT

When man fell in the Garden of Eden and ceded the right to governing the earth to Satan, the devil established his government on earth, and he now reigns over the kingdoms of men. Genesis 3:15 highlights how God puts enmity between the serpent (the devil) and the woman, and he declares that the seed of the woman will crush the head of the devil, and the devil will strike his heel. The head of Satan speaks of his headship, authority, leadership, government, and dominion, while the heel of the seed of the woman refers to the stability or balance of his body.

The Word of God became flesh, was born by a woman (Mary), and he dwelt among humans to deliver the sons of men from sin, death, and the dominion of the wicked. When he died and rose from the dead, he disarmed and took from the devil the authority he stole from man and he gave it to his body, the church, to exercise on earth. This is why the church is the only entity accredited by heaven to exercise divine authority and enforce God's will and agenda on earth.

We Christians (members of the universal body of Christ), are the law enforcement agents of God on earth, and we have the legal authority to challenge, resist, and rebuke the devil by the word of God and prayer. Christ gave us divine warrant and authority to destroy the works of the wicked, enforce God's judicial counsel for humankind, and birth his will.

For this reason, Satan is using every possible means to attack the church and cause it to be unstable or fall as retaliation for what Christ did to him. He mostly uses occasion and accusation as weapons.

Whenever a window of opportunity opens, he takes advantage of it to vex, incite, provoke, tempt, or influence a believer to do something that he can use to discredit, accuse, or prosecute the person in the courtroom of heaven (Ecc.9:11, Rev.12:10).

When we do certain things, it causes our hedge of protection to collapse. Satan always provokes, entices, or seduces believers to do things that form legal grounds in the spirit realm that he uses as basis for prosecuting, resisting, attacking, or hindering us. 2 Corinthians 2:11 talks about the schemes of the devil that allow him to outsmart people.

The Bible declares in Matthew 22:29 that we fall in error for two reasons. The first is that we do not know the scriptures, and the latter is we do not know the power of God. The devil uses our ignorance to manipulate and take advantage of us. My people are destroyed from lack of knowledge, says the prophet Hosea (Hos. 4:6).

Zechariah 3:1-7 recounts how Joshua the high priest stood before the angel of the Lord, and Satan stood at his right hand side to accuse him. Right hand speaks of power and authority, and for Satan to stand at his right hand side means Joshua lost his authority by reason of the filthy garment he was wearing. Verse 4 says the angel of the Lord told him (Joshua) that his sin was taken away, while verse 7 talks about the angel instructing him to walk in obedience and keep his requirements.

It stands to reason that Joshua's disobedience and sin brought the filthy garments on him and caused him to lose his authority. Satan took advantage of it and used it as legal ground to accuse, discredit, and resist him before the angel of the Lord.

RULES OF ENGAGEMENT

There are things we do that give the wicked legal ground to resist us in the spirit.

Satan has no power over us as Christians because of the finished work of Christ on the cross. He's not as powerful as many think, only that he uses deception, occasion and accusation to gain advantage over us. He knows the rules very well and he understands how the spiritual legal system operates. He capitalizes on our ignorance and uses it to manipulate us.

Christ took the lawful authority that man gave to Satan from him and gave it to the church, his body. Christ is the head and his body is the church. His heel is a metaphoric expression that speaks of his body (the church, because one's heel is in the body), and that is why Satan is brutally attacking the church.

The only place Satan can strike by divine order is Christ's body (heel), according to Genesis 3:15. To do this, he devises strategy and establishes legal ground on which he stands to launch deadly onslaughts against the body of Christ. The Lord Jesus said in Matthew 16:18 that he will build his church and the gates of hell will not overcome it. No matter the aggression of Satan and his cohorts against the church, they will not prevail over us. Romans 16:20 says that God will crush Satan under our feet.

The rules of engagement outline the "dos" and "don'ts" and establish the lines and boundaries according to the legal system of heaven, as revealed in the word of God. It defines the circumstances under which some actions that are considered illegal could be legally acceptable in the courtroom of heaven. It also establishes grounds that either favor or condemn certain action. Understanding these rules and complying with them gives us advantage in prayer.

UNDERSTANDING the Art of Prayer (Revisited)

During Jesus' earthly ministry, he did and said so many things that were considered provocative and unlawful by the religious leaders of his time. John 8:28-29 reveals that he did what pleased the Father and says what the Father taught him. In John 12:49, the Lord himself said that the Father gave him command on what to say and how to say it. Knowing what the Father approves gave him the right to do what no other person could imagine or do.

Another good example is when Miriam and Aaron spoke against Moses because of his wife. The Bible says the anger of the Lord burned against both of them, but when judgment came, it affected only Miriam. How could two people do something and only one get punished? The reason is because Aaron had immunity by reason of his priestly office and garments that set him apart (Num.12:1-15).

This whole thing is about understanding biblical truths, concepts, and principles. God does nothing outside his word; he only respects principles. Your understanding of this rule gives you the upper hand in prayer. Knowing who you are and what is scripturally acceptable, how the wicked operate and the things that give them advantage in the spirit, and how to break their legal ground and dismiss their charges, would make you very effective in prayer.

You can't bind or kill Satan because his end has been decided by the Godhead. He has been sentenced by the court of heaven to eternal damnation and there is nothing anyone can do to change that. Until his time comes to an end, he will continue his evil works on earth and deceive many people.

RULES OF ENGAGEMENT

The mandate Christ gave to the church is not to bind or kill Satan, because it is legally impossible to do that according to scripture (Rev.20:1-10).

When Christ died and rose from the dead, the Godhead exalted him to the highest place of authority and gave him the name that is above every other name, and at the mention of his name, every knee should bow in heaven, on earth, and under the earth, and that every tongue confesses that Jesus Christ is Lord to the glory of the Father (Phi.2:6-11). Christ gave these three dimensions of authority, which the Father gave him to the church and he expect us to exercise it in his name.

2 Peter 1:3 says he gives us everything that pertains to life and godliness to enjoy, in proportion to the measure of the knowledge we have about him. Revelation knowledge produces faith (Rom.10:17), and faith is a vital factor in prayer (Mk.11:23, Heb.11:6). With proper knowledge of who we are in Christ and what we have, how to use it, who the enemy is, his modes of operation, and how to deal with him will give you the upper hand in prayer.

Learn more about biblical truths, concepts and principles in the written word of God, and you will understand the rules of engagement in relation to spiritual warfare and intercession. The code is locked up in the Bible. Read in between the lines and you will unlock it.

BIBLICAL TRUTHS

This is the real facts from God's perspective. It is constant, firm, and reliable (it never changes). There are many things the human eyes and mind cannot see or comprehend, and the fact we can't see it does not mean it doesn't exist. The Lord sees what we don't see and he knows what we don't know. When he speaks, he says it the way it really is.

BIBLICAL CONCEPTS

These are notions revealed in the Bible that give us insight to spiritual things. There are key concepts in the Bible that we have to understand, and knowing them gives you confidence. The following are few examples: covenant, faith, sin, redemption, justification, salvation, baptism, confession, anointing, etc.

BIBLICAL PRINCIPLES

These never change. They work everywhere. The principle of sowing and reaping, giving and receiving, birth and death, and day and night are constant. Understanding biblical principles helps you to know how God works. The reason father Abraham addressed God the way he did is because he knew how God works.

CHAPTER 5

HINDRANCES TO PRAYER

God's eternal love for humanity always moves him to interfere in human affairs, but he cannot do it without cooperation from mankind through prayer. Otherwise, he would violate the principles that he established in the beginning when he entrusted mankind with the authority to govern the earth. Prayers authorize God to work on earth, but when the rules of engagement and divine order are violated, our prayers can be hindered. Below is a list of some hindrances to prayer.

IGNORANCE

Ignorance is no excuse! There is a story in Mark 9:14-29 that illustrates this point. The passage shows how a certain man brought his son who was possessed by a deaf and mute spirit to Jesus' disciples for deliverance, but they could not heal him. This lead to an argument between the teachers of the law and the disciples of Jesus.

UNDERSTANDING the Art of Prayer (Revisited)

As soon as the people saw Jesus, they went and greeted him. Jesus asked his disciples what they were arguing about. The father of the sick boy answered, "Teacher, I brought you my son, who is possessed by a spirit that has robbed him of speech. Whenever it seizes him, it throws him to the ground. He foams at the mouth, gnashes his teeth, and becomes rigid. I asked your disciples to drive out the spirit, but they could not."

Jesus replied, "O faithless generation, how long must I be with you? How long must I put up with you? Bring the boy to me." So they brought the boy to him. But when the evil spirit saw Jesus, it threw the boy into a convulsion, and he fell to the ground, and rolled about, foaming at the mouth. Jesus asked the boy's father how long he has been like that. "From childhood," he answered. "It has often thrown him into fire or water to kill him. But if you can do anything, take pity on us and help us." "If you can," Jesus said, "All things are possible for one who believes."

Immediately the father of the boy cried out and said, "I believe; help me overcome my unbelief!" When Jesus saw that a crowd was running to the scene, he rebuked the evil spirit, "You deaf and mute spirit, I command you to come out of him and never enter him again." The spirit screamed, convulsed him violently, and came out of the boy. Jesus then took him by his hand and lifted him to his feet, and he arose. When Jesus went inside, his disciples asked him why they could not cast out the evil spirit. He replied, "This kind can come forth by nothing, but by prayer and fasting."

As mentioned earlier, ignorance is no excuse. What you know about prayer determines the effectiveness of your prayer.

HINDRANCES TO PRAYER

Had the disciples knew the importance of fasting and prayer in deliverance, they would have successfully delivered the boy from the evil spirit that held him captive.

There are so many things we ignore about prayer that impact our prayer life negatively. Hosea 4:6 says that we are destroyed from lack of knowledge. Knowledge is power. The knowledge you have about the things that make prayer work could take your prayer life to a new dimension. Learn more about prayer, know more about what makes it work, and you will produce more results in prayer.

The disciples asked him why they couldn't drive the evil spirit out, because they realized there was something they were ignorant of that affected them negatively. Knowing what Jesus knew about prayer would make them produce the same result that Jesus produced. And knowing that the problem they were facing required fasting and prayer for them to gain advantage and prevail would make them very effective if they practice what they knew.

SIN

The Bible declares in 2 Chronicle 7:14 that if my people who are called by name will humble themselves and pray, and seek my face and turn from their wicked ways, I will hear from heaven and forgive their sin, and heal their land. We notice in this passage that for God to hear and answer the prayer of his people, certain conditions must be met. Otherwise, their prayer won't be answered, because God honors his word and does things according to the principles he put in place. Once the principle is violated, he cannot go against his word and grant his people their needs.

UNDERSTANDING the Art of Prayer (Revisited)

Hosea 7:1-2 says when God would have healed Israel, the sin of Ephraim appeared and the iniquity of Samaria was revealed, for they deal falsely, the thief breaks in, and the bandit raids outside. Their evil deeds engulf them and they are always before my face, says the Lord. No matter how hard the people cried, as long as their sins engulfed them and clouded their path, their prayers could not be answered. Sin and iniquity are the number one hindrance to answered prayer. The psalmist says, if I had cherished sin in my heart, the Lord would not have listened. He said this because sin hinders prayer from being answered.

Indeed, the Lord's hand is not too short to save, and His ear is not too deaf to hear. But your iniquities have built barriers between you and your God, and your sins have made Him hide His face from you so that He does not listen.
(Is.59:1-2 HCSB)

God said in Isaiah 1:15-18 that when we lift up our hands in prayer, he will turn his face away and he won't hear us. And though we make many prayers, he won't listen, for our hands are full of blood. "Wash and make yourselves clean. Take your evil deeds out of my sight and stop doing wrong. Come now, and let us reason together," says the Lord. "Though your sins are like scarlet, they shall be as white as snow; though they are red like crimson, they shall become like wool."

Sin is a killer disease that can cut us off from God. No matter how long and how hard we pray, sin can hinder our prayers from being answered. All God required from us is to repent, confess, and turn from our wrongdoings, and he will forgive and clean us from all unrighteousness.

HINDRANCES TO PRAYER

If we say that we have no sin, we deceive ourselves, and the truth is not in us. If we confess our sins, He is faithful and just to forgive us our sins and to cleanse us from all unrighteousness. If we say that we have not sinned, we make Him a liar, and His word is not in us.
(1 Jn.1:8-10 NKJV)

To say we have no sin in us is a lie because of the weakness of our body. All the Lord expects from us is to acknowledge our sin and to turn away from it. For whoever sins is a slave to sin, according to scripture (Jn.8:34).

1 John 2:1 says we should not sin. But if anyone does sin, we have a defense attorney who speaks to the Father on our behalf, Jesus Christ, the righteous one, who died for our sins and rose for our justification. By his precious blood, we are cleansed. For without the shedding of blood, there is no forgiveness of sin (Heb.9:22). The sacrifice has been made, and the blood is available. All we have to do is acknowledge our sins, confess them, and obtain forgiveness in the name of Jesus Christ.

WRONG MOTIVE

We serve a God who judges the heart or motive of our actions. He said to the prophet Samuel in 1 Samuel 16:7 that he does not look at the outward appearance but on the heart.

Genesis 38:6-10 recounts how Judah got a wife for Er, his firstborn, and her name was Tamar. But Er was wicked in the sight of the Lord, so he put him to death. Then Judah asked his second son Onan to sleep with his late brother's wife and raise up offspring for his brother.

UNDERSTANDING the Art of Prayer (Revisited)

But Onan knew that the child will not be his. So whenever he slept with his brother's wife, he would spill his seed on the ground so he would not provide offspring for his brother. The Lord put him to death also, because his act was wicked.

This shows that God always searches our motives in whatever we do, including prayer. And when the motive is wrong, he won't grant it, for he is righteous in justice and just in righteousness. Romans 8:27 says God searches the heart to know what is in the mind.

Now a man named Ananias, together with his wife Sapphira, also sold a piece of property. With his wife's full knowledge he kept back part of the money for himself, but brought the rest and put it at the apostles' feet. Then Peter said, "Ananias, how is it that Satan has so filled your heart that you have lied to the Holy Spirit and have kept for yourself some of the money you received for the land? Didn't it belong to you before it was sold? And after it was sold, wasn't the money at your disposal? What made you think of doing such a thing? You have not lied to men but to God." When Ananias heard this, he fell down and died. And great fear seized all who heard what had happened. Then the young men came forward, wrapped up his body, and carried him out and buried him. About three hours later his wife came in, not knowing what had happened. Peter asked her, "Tell me, is this the price you and Ananias got for the land?" "Yes," she said, "that is the price." Peter said to her, "How could you agree to test the Spirit of the Lord? Look! The feet of the men who buried your husband are at the door, and they will carry you out also." At that moment she fell down at his feet and died. Then the young men came in and, finding her dead, carried her out and buried her beside her husband. Great fear seized the whole church and all who heard about these events.
(Acts 5:1-11 NIV)

HINDRANCES TO PRAYER

Ananias and his wife Sapphira died because their motive was not right before God. They had an ulterior motive as they sold some property, kept part of the money for themselves, brought the rest to the apostles, and pretended it was all the money. Perhaps they did this to gain respect from the people, but it was a wicked act in God's sight. Everyone may think they have done a noble act, but the Lord who searches the motive of every action knew their motivation was wrong. So he put them to death, as he did to Onan the son of Judah.

The preceding chapter tells how Barnabas had sold a piece of property and brought the money to the apostles. It was then distributed to the people according to their needs so that there was no needy person among them (Acts 4:34-37). Every action is fueled by a motive, and there could never be motivation without a motive. A friend once said, "Behind every move we make, lies a motive."

In the sight of the Lord, motive is prized over action. This is why James 4:3 says you do not receive when you ask because you ask with wrong motives, to spend it on your passions. Therefore, a wrong motive can cause God not to answer our prayers. To have a good motive, check the main reason you are making the request. Good reason produces a positive motive that fuels your actions.

GOD REFUSING TO ANSWER

Apart from sins and wrong motives, there are many other reasons why God may decide not to answer some prayers. The first is when what we are asking for is not his original will or plan.

UNDERSTANDING the Art of Prayer (Revisited)

Scripture declares in Ephesians 1:11 that God works out everything in conformity with the purpose of his will. This means that before God will answer your prayer, it must be in alignment with his will. Knowing the will of God for every situation is very important when cultivating a consistent prayer life.

Matthew 26:36-44 describes how the Lord Jesus said his soul was overwhelmed with sorrow to the point of death. He bowed with his face to the ground and prayed that the Father would take the cup from him. Even though he persistently cried out about the same thing, the Father did not grant his request, because it was against his will. The will of God was that Christ should die for the sins of humanity, but Jesus didn't want to go to the cross and was praying for the Father to change the plan.

The same thing happened to the apostle Paul when he was given a thorn in the flesh to keep him from becoming proud because of the abundant revelation God gave him about Christ and the church. He prayed three times that the messenger of Satan sent to torment him in the flesh might depart, but God did not answer his prayer because, granting his desire might do him more harm than good (2 Co.12:7-9).

Therefore do not pray for this people, nor lift up a cry or prayer for them, nor make intercession to Me; for I will not hear you. Do you not see what they do in the cities of Judah and in the streets of Jerusalem? The children gather wood, the fathers kindle the fire, and the women knead dough, to make cakes for the queen of heaven; and they pour out drink offerings to other gods, that they may provoke Me to anger. Do they provoke Me to anger?" says the Lord.

HINDRANCES TO PRAYER

"Do they not provoke themselves, to the shame of their own faces?
(Jer. 7:16-19 NKJV)

They have turned back to the iniquities of their forefathers, who refused to hear my words. They have gone after other gods to serve them. The house of Israel and the house of Judah have broken my covenant that I made with their fathers. Therefore, thus says the Lord, behold, I am bringing disaster upon them that they cannot escape. Though they cry to me, I will not listen to them. Then the cities of Judah and the inhabitants of Jerusalem will go and cry to the gods to whom they make offerings, but they cannot save them in the time of their trouble. For your gods have become as many as your cities, O Judah, and as many as the streets of Jerusalem are the altars you have set up to shame, altars to make offerings to Baal. Therefore do not pray for this people, or lift up a cry or prayer on their behalf, for I will not listen when they call to me in the time of their trouble.
(Jer. 11:10-14 ESV)

We observe in the above passages how the Lord instructed his servant the prophet Jeremiah not to pray for his people. Do not pray for this people or weep for them, and do not intercede in their favor, for I will not listen to you, says the Lord. For God to tell him not to intercede for his people means that Jeremiah was going to pray to God for the land, so the Lord had to stop him.

Chapter 14:11-12 shows how the Lord asked him (Jeremiah) not to pray for the well-being of the people. Though they fast, I will not hear their cry, and though they offer burnt offering and grain offering, I will not accept them, says the Lord.

DEMONIC OPERATION

From the moment Adam ceded the right and authority to governing the earth to Satan, the devil and his cohorts have ruled over the affairs of the kingdom of men. And since prayer is the primary means by which humans give God authorization to interfere in the affairs of mankind, demons orchestrate things to hinder it. To do this, they seek occasion among humans and then use it to establish legal ground on which they stand to perpetuate their wicked agenda.

Daniel 4:34-35 declares that God's kingdom and dominion is everlasting. And that none is like him, for he does as he pleases with the powers of heaven and the people of the earth. No one can stop him or question his action. Nonetheless, he respects principles and does nothing outside his word.

Once the wicked establishes legal grounds in a region, they use it to exercise control over the place, as we observe in the case of the prophet Daniel, who fasted and prayed twenty-one days while in Babylon (Dan.10:2-13). Although God heard his prayer from the very day he prayed, he could not receive what he asked of the Lord, because the angel God sent to respond to his prayer was blocked and detained by the prince of Persia.

The prince of Persia is the demonic entity or principality (Eph.6:12) that ruled over the region of the kingdom of Persia where Daniel lived at the time. And because the right to governing the place was given to that principality, it controlled the spiritual gateway and territory of the region, so that nothing came in or went out of the region without its permission.

HINDRANCES TO PRAYER

When the angel bringing the response to Daniel's prayer entered the jurisdiction of the Persian kingdom, the spirit that ruled over it intercepted and captured him. Daniel's persistent fasting and prayer provoked heavenly reinforcement, and the angel Michael was sent to release the messenger of God that carried the response to Daniel's prayer from demonic custody.

The detention of the angel delayed Daniel's miracle. Had Daniel not persisted in prayer, he would not have received answer to his prayer even though God granted him his desire. Demonic operation sometimes blocks prayers from being answered.

Since spirits can't operate on earth without bodies, they use human bodies to carry out their agenda. But they cannot use anyone's body unless the person yields himself to them by doing things that give demonic spirits the right to influence, incite, manipulate or control him or her. The same way God uses humans to advance his will on earth, Satan does the same thing.

The Lord Jesus said in Revelation 3:20 that he stands at the door and knocks, and if anyone hears his voice and opens, he will come in and eat with the person. God will not enter someone heart unless the person invites him by accepting his offer for salvation and confessing his lordship (Rom.10:9-10). This is so because he (God) gave mankind free will to choose whatever we want (Gen.2:16-17), and he won't violate his principles.

Just as we do things that cause God to use us in accomplishing his counsel in the earth, there are things people do that also give Satan free access to use them in advancing his wicked agenda in this world.

UNDERSTANDING the Art of Prayer (Revisited)

There is a continuous battle over our body as light, which represents God, and darkness, which represents Satan, want to use us in fulfilling their agenda on earth, for no spirit can operate in this world without a body.

When the spirit that controls a nation, region, or house is demonic, it can intercept, control or determine what happens at the place unless it is bound. This is why Christ gave us power to bind every strong man and overturn their works wherever we dwell.

Luke 11:21-22 declares that when a strong man, fully armed, guards his house, his properties are safe. But when someone stronger than him attacks and overpowers him, he strips him of his weapons and carries off his belongings. This is why Mark 3:27 says that no one can enter into a strong man's house and take away his possessions unless he first binds him. Whenever you enter a region, scan it in the Spirit and use your divine authority to change the spiritual climate over the place by breaking every legal ground that the wicked have over the zone, take dominion, and then superimpose God's reign and will over the territory (I'll expand on this in my other book, *Strategic Prayer*, under the heading, "Binding the strong man").

The prophet Zechariah relates how God showed him Joshua the high priest standing before the angel of the Lord, and Satan standing at his right hand side to accuse him. As earlier mentioned, right hand speaks of power and authority, and for Satan to stand at his right hand means that Joshua the high priest lost his legal authority because of sin, since he was wearing a filthy garment. As a result, Satan gained advantage over him and resisted his intercession.

HINDRANCES TO PRAYER

As long as Joshua had the dirty garment on, the devil would resist his prayer and hinder the response no matter how much or hard he prayed (Zech.3:1-7). The only way out is to deal with the legalities Satan is using by deploying the blood of Jesus. It could be sin, covenant, curses, ignorance, or anything that gives the wicked legal ground to operate so that your prayer may not be hindered.

Demons have no power over us apart from that which we give them through words or actions. Ephesians 4:26-27 says in your anger do not sin. Don't let the sun go down while you are still angry, and do not give the devil a foothold. When you give Satan a grip, he uses it against you in so many ways.

Joshua the high priest lost his authority and gave the wicked a foothold through sin. This cost him his immunity and gave the devil the lawful right to exert upon him. If you feel like your prayers have been delayed or hindered because of demonic orchestration, first deal with any possible legal grounds they are operating from, and then address the spirit behind it by exercising your divine authority in Christ.

WRONG TIMING

God works with time. "There is a time for everything and a season for every purpose or activity," says the Teacher (Eccl.3:1). Verse 11 of the same chapter declares God made everything beautiful in its time, that is, in the time of the thing (for everything has its time). Knowing how God works is very important in a walk with the Holy Spirit, because the Lord does things according to his own calendar. Divine timing differs from human timing.

UNDERSTANDING the Art of Prayer (Revisited)

2 Peter 3:8 says a day is like a thousand years with the Lord, and a thousand years is like a day. His ways are not our ways; as the heavens are higher than the earth, so are the ways of the Lord higher than ours. The Bible talks about the men of Issachar who understood the signs of the times and knew what Israel should do. This gave them advantage and puts their relatives under their command.

Luke 19:41-44 tells how the Lord Jesus saw the city of Jerusalem and started to weep over it, because it did not know its time of visitation. If you're a good Bible student, you'll notice that Jesus didn't cry about everything. There were few instances in the Bible when Jesus cried, and this was one of them. He cried over Jerusalem because it did not understand the time it was in, neither did it understand what could have brought it peace. Their long expected Messiah was in their midst, but the people of Jerusalem could not recognize him. They missed their time of visitation, and went through hard times, as we notice in the passage.

He approached and saw the city, He wept over it, saying, "If you knew this day what would bring peace—but now it is hidden from your eyes. For the days will come on you when your enemies will build an embankment against you, surround you, and hem you in on every side. They will crush you and your children within you to the ground, and they will not leave one stone on another in you, because you did not recognize the time of your visitation."
(Lk.19:41-44 HCSB)

Had they known their time of visitation, they would have positioned themselves, and made the most of the time for a better life. When you understand divine timing and know how to discern the right time for things, you will always work wonders through prayer.

HINDRANCES TO PRAYER

The passage in 1 Chronicles 14:8-17 highlights the importance of understanding and walking according to God's timing. When the Philistines heard that David had been anointed over Israel, they went in full force to capture him. But David heard about it, and he went out to meet them. He inquired of the Lord whether he should go out against the Philistines, and whether God will deliver them into his hand. The Lord answered him, "Go, I will deliver them into your hands." With this in mind, David and his troops went up to Baal-Perazim and defeated the Philistines there.

David said, "God has broken through my enemies by my hand, like a bursting flood." So he called the place Baal-Perazim. Sometime later, the Philistines attacked and raided the valley. So David again asked of the Lord whether he should attack them immediately. But God said to him, "Do not go up after them, but circle around and attack them near the poplar trees. As soon as you hear the sound of matching in the tops of the poplar trees, go out and attack for God has gone out before you to strike down the army of the Philistines." David did as God commanded him, and they struck down the Philistines army from Gibeon to Gazer. Then David's fame spread everywhere, and the Lord made all the nations fear him.

You will notice in the passage that David's victory was due to his ability to inquire of the Lord for direction and his obedience to divine instruction. God commanded him to wait until he hears the sound of matching feet in the tops of the trees before going out to attack his enemies. Had he gone out to attack the Philistines before the appointed time, he would have faced them alone and lost the battle, because God would not have gone with him to the battlefield.

UNDERSTANDING the Art of Prayer (Revisited)

The Bible declares in Psalm 102:13 that God will arise and have compassion on Zion because the set time to favor her, the appointed time, has come. According to Ecclesiastes 9:11, the race is not to the swift or the battle to the strong, nor does food come to the wise or wealth to the brilliant or favor to the learned, but time and chances happen to them all.

This is what the Lord Almighty, the God of Israel, says to all those I carried into exile from Jerusalem to Babylon: "Build houses and settle down; plant gardens and eat what they produce. Marry and have sons and daughters; find wives for your sons and give your daughters in marriage, so that they too may have sons and daughters. Increase in number there; do not decrease. Also, seek the peace and prosperity of the city to which I have carried you into exile. Pray to the Lord for it, because if it prospers, you too will prosper." Yes, this is what the Lord Almighty, the God of Israel, says: "Do not let the prophets and diviners among you deceive you. Do not listen to the dreams you encourage them to have. They are prophesying lies to you in my name. I have not sent them," declares the Lord. This is what the Lord says: "When seventy years are completed for Babylon, I will come to you and fulfill my gracious promise to bring you back to this place. For I know the plans I have for you," declares the Lord, "plans to prosper you and not to harm you, plans to give you hope and a future. Then you will call upon me and come and pray to me, and I will listen to you. You will seek me and find me when you seek me with all your heart. I will be found by you," declares the Lord, "and will bring you back from captivity. I will gather you from all the nations and places where I have banished you," declares the Lord, "and will bring you back to the place from which I carried you into exile."
(Jer. 29:4-14 NIV)

HINDRANCES TO PRAYER

The passage above places more emphasis on the significance of divine timing and how it affects our prayers being answered. When the people of God went to exile from Jerusalem to Babylon, some thought they could return home anytime soon. God had to make them understand by the letter the prophet Jeremiah sent that no amount of prayer or sacrifice would make him change his mind about their return from exile before the seventy years he assigned them. His plan was when seventy years were completed in Babylon, he would visit them and fulfill his gracious promise to bring them back to their home land.

Then you will call upon me and come and pray to me, and I will listen to you. You will seek me and find me when you seek me with all your heart. I will be found by you and will bring you back from captivity," declares the Lord. When you do not have proper understanding of divine timing, you will struggle in prayer.

LACK OF FAITH

Hebrews 11:6 says without faith it is impossible to please God, for anyone who comes to him must believe he exists and that he rewards those who earnestly seek him. Faith comes by hearing the word of God or believing what scripture says about him. No one can receive anything from God unless he believes God exists and that he can do what he is asking him for.

In his model for prayer, the Lord Jesus asked us to say, "Our Father in heaven, hallowed be your name…" It is required that we accept God as father, and there is no way we can accept him as our father unless we believe he exists.

Everyone praying to God must believe he lives and that he has the power to do whatever you are asking for in prayer. Without faith, you cannot receive anything from God.

Mark 11:23 declares that if anyone says to the mountain to move and does not doubt, but believes that what he says will happen, he will receive whatever he asks. Lack of faith in what you ask God for can hinder your prayer from being answered.

According to James 1:6-8, whoever asks God for something must believe and not doubt, for he who doubts is like a wave of the sea, blown and tossed by the wind. Let such a person not think that he will receive anything from the Lord; he is a double-minded person, unstable in whatever he does.

The first thing Jesus said about his disciples that could not cast out the evil spirit from the boy who was possessed with a deaf and mute spirit is that they lack faith. "O faithless generation, how long must I be with you? How long must I put up with you?" (Mk.9:19). The reason they had no faith was because of their ignorance. Had they known what it took to move that mountain, and to do it the right way, they would have produced the same result Jesus produced through prayer.

The Bible declares in Romans 10:10 that faith comes from hearing the word, and that the message is heard through the word of God. To increase your faith, study what the Bible says about the issue you are facing, and deploy the appropriate weapon in prayer to deal with it. When you understand the promises of God concerning a thing and believe in it, it releases the faith you need to deal with the thing in prayer.

CHAPTER 6

MECHANISM OF PRAYER

The mechanism of prayer deals with how prayer works, and the different dynamics or factors involved in the whole process. There is so much misunderstanding in the body of Christ regarding this concept due to diverse points of view — doctrines and beliefs that people have about it. Any time I teach on this subject, many people frequently ask about the role God the Father, Jesus the Son, and the Holy Spirit play when we pray.

As we were discussing this subject in one of my meetings, a certain woman asked, "Don't you think God the Father could sometimes be mad at us for asking Jesus or the Holy Spirit things, rather than him?"

At first, I didn't understand her question. So I asked if she could explain what she meant by the Father being mad at us for asking Jesus or the Holy Spirit things rather than him.

Then she said, "People often pray to Jesus or the Holy Spirit when they are supposed to direct their prayers to the Father.

UNDERSTANDING the Art of Prayer (Revisited)

The Father is the head and he should be given the first place in all things whether in prayer or worship. Directing our prayers to Jesus or the Holy Spirit means we are exalting them above the Godhead. I don't think it is right." She said in conclusion.

I laughed quietly, and then motioned with my hands for the people to be quiet as few others who shared her point of view raised their voices in support to what she said, while others responded differently. The class was divided as each person tried to share their view on the subject. Having gained their attention, I started by explaining the concept of Father, Son, and Spirit in the Godhead before speaking on their roles in answering prayers.

In my book *The Oneness of God*, formerly published as "Fullness of the Deity," I explained that God is one eternal being. For the benefit of those who haven't read it, below is an excerpt from the book.

"The Godhead is one eternal Spirit whose power and divine nature constitute the fullness of his being in eternity past (Rom.1:20). The beginning began when he allowed his eternal power to subsist as individual being, and it subsisted in him as the Word and Spirit.

To be precise, the individual existence of God's Word and Spirit commenced the beginning of God's works. That is why scripture declares that in the beginning was the Word (Jn.1:1) and that he is the firstborn over all creation (Col.1:15). Proverbs 8:22 says he was brought forth as the first of God's works, before his deeds of old, while verse 23 declares he was appointed from eternity, and verse 30 adds that he was the craftsman at God's side.

MECHANISM OF PRAYER

The reason for this is that God begot his creative power in eternity as his Word not as a Son, to be with him by allowing him to subsist as individual being. The subsistence of God's Word and Spirit in the Godhead marked the commencement of God's works. The Word, Spirit, and essence of God constitute the fullness of his being in the beginning.

At the appointed time, God sent his Word to die for the sins of humanity. The Word became flesh, died on the cross, rose from the dead and ascended bodily to the right hand throne of God. There he obtained the Holy Spirit from the Father, who also made him both Lord and Christ (Acts 2:32-36).

The incarnate Word, being one in essence with the Godhead, came together with the Holy Spirit in the glorified body of Jesus Christ to form a single person. For this reason, scripture declares in Colossians 2:9 that in Christ dwells the fullness of the Godhead bodily — because the fundamental constituents of God are his Word, Spirit, and essence, and they all dwell in Christ in bodily form.

The bodily presence of Christ in the throne room of heaven caused a change in the existence of God from "God, his Word and Spirit" to "God the Father," "Jesus his Son" and "the Holy Spirit." This means that the Father, Son, and Spirit in the Godhead does not signify three separates gods as some think, and neither does it indicates different manifestations, titles, roles, or functions that the one true God assumed at diverse times in history or the different modes through which Jesus manifested to humanity as others believe.

UNDERSTANDING the Art of Prayer (Revisited)

On the contrary, it signifies the highest level of self-revelation of the one and only true eternal God who now exists simultaneously as Father, Son, and Holy Spirit because of the church – the body and bride of Christ. The Father, Son and Spirit exist simultaneously as one in essence but distinct in being.

The Father and Son relationship between the creator of heaven and earth and Jesus of Nazareth is due to the oneness that has existed between them both from the beginning and the eternal plan of the Godhead that was accomplished through Jesus. This means that though he made himself nothing by taking on the very nature of a servant to redeem humankind, he is one with the Godhead in essence based on his pre-existence as the Word of God.

The Godhead is the Father over his works (the visionary and possessor of all things); everything begins and ends in him. Jesus Christ inherited all things from the Godhead (Heb.1:2), who also made him both Lord and Christ (administrator). The Holy Spirit is the sole executor of all divine counsel (facilitator), which means that the Godhead now exists as Father – visionary, Son – administrator, and Spirit – facilitator (Matt.28:19-20, 1 Co.12:4-6, 2 Co.13:14, Lk.3:21-22), because of Christ." (For more information on this, please go to my book *The Oneness of God*).

In his model for prayer, the Lord Jesus says that when you pray, say, "Our Father in heaven, hallowed be your name." Verse 6 of the same passage says when you pray, go into your room, shut the door and pray to your Father who is unseen. And your Father who sees in secret will reward you openly. Verse 8 declares that the Father knows what we need before we ask him (Matt.6:6-9).

MECHANISM OF PRAYER

According to scriptures, Peter and John were arrested and brought before the Sanhedrin to be questioned for healing a man lame from birth that the people carried each day to the temple gate called Beautiful so that he could beg from the people going into the temple.

Having been arrested and brought before the council, the Sanhedrin asked, "By what power or what name did you do this?" Peter, speaking by the Holy Spirit, said, "Rulers and elders of the people! If we are being called to account today for an act of kindness shown to a cripple and are asked how he was healed, then know this, you and all the people of Israel: It is by the name of Jesus Christ of Nazareth, who you crucified but who God raised from the dead, that this man stand before you healed."

The passage says since they could see the man who had been healed standing there, there was nothing they could say. "What are we going to do with these men?" They asked. "Everybody living in Jerusalem knows that they have done an outstanding miracle, and we cannot deny it. But to stop this thing from spreading any further among the people, we must warn these men to speak no longer to anyone in this name."

They called Peter and John in again and commanded them not to speak or teach at all in the name of Jesus. Being threatened and warned by the Sanhedrin not to speak or teach at all in the name of Jesus, they reported the matter to their own people. Verse 24 declares that when the people heard it, they raised their voices together in prayer to God (Acts 4:1-31).

UNDERSTANDING the Art of Prayer (Revisited)

Acts 4:12 declares salvation is found in no one else, for there is no other name under heaven given to mankind by which we must be saved. The name of Jesus is the only name accredited by heaven that guarantees answered prayer, and salvation amongst humans.

There is only one God and one mediator between God and humanity, the man Christ Jesus, according to scripture (1 Tim.2:5). Philippians 2:6-11 says that though he was in very nature God, he did not consider equality with God something to be used to his own advantage, but emptied himself by taking the form of a servant, being born in the likeness of men. And being found in appearance as a man, he humbled himself by becoming obedient to the point of death, even death on a cross.

Therefore God exalted him to the highest place and gave him the name that is above every name, that at the name of Jesus every knee should bow, in heaven and on earth and under the earth, and every tongue confess that Jesus Christ is Lord, to the glory of God the Father. This is why the Lord said in John 15:16b that whatever we ask the Father in his name, he will give to us. He also said in John 14:13 that he will do whatever we ask in his name, so that the Father may be glorified in the Son. Verse 14 says if we ask him anything in his name, he will do it.

At that time you won't need to ask me for anything. I tell you the truth, you will ask the Father directly, and he will grant your request because you use my name. You haven't done this before. Ask, using my name, and you will receive, and you will have abundant joy. I have spoken of these matters in figures of speech, but soon I will stop speaking figuratively and will tell you plainly all about the Father.

MECHANISM OF PRAYER

Then you will ask in my name. I'm not saying I will ask the Father on your behalf, for the Father himself loves you dearly because you love me and believe that I came from God. Yes, I came from the Father into the world, and now I will leave the world and return to the Father.
(Jn.16:23-28 NLT)

I still have many things to tell you, but you can't bear them now. When the Spirit of truth comes, He will guide you into all the truth. For He will not speak on His own, but He will speak whatever He hears. He will also declare to you what is to come. He will glorify Me, because He will take from what is Mine and declare it to you. Everything the Father has is Mine. This is why I told you that He takes from what is Mine and will declare it to you.
(Jn.16:12-14 HCSB)

The Father, Son, and Spirit is one God. Whether you say heavenly Father, Lord Jesus, or Holy Spirit in your prayer, it doesn't matter, because God is one. Only that we need a name, and the only name given to humanity that guarantees us answered prayer is the name of Jesus Christ of Nazareth. This name is above every other name in heaven, on earth, and beneath the earth. Do it in the name of Jesus, and your prayers will produce the result you desire.

I appeal to you, brothers, by our Lord Jesus Christ and by the love of the Spirit, to strive together with me in your prayers to God on my behalf, that I may be delivered from the unbelievers in Judea, and that my service for Jerusalem may be acceptable to the saints, so that by God's will I may come to you with joy and be refreshed in your company. May the God of peace be with you all. Amen.
(Rom.15:30-33 ESV)

UNDERSTANDING the Art of Prayer (Revisited)

On another occasion, someone quoted the passage in Revelation 8:3-4 that talks about an angel with a golden incense burner that came and stood at the altar. The angel was given much incense to mix with the prayers of God's people as an offering on the golden altar that is before the throne. The smoke of the incense mixed with the prayer of the saints and ascended up to God from the angel's hand. Then the angel took the censer and filled it with fire from the altar and threw it on the earth, and there were voices, thunder, lightning, and an earthquake.

Then the individual asked me whether angels, Mary the mother of Jesus, the Cherubim, the twenty-four elders in the courtroom of heaven, etc. also play strategic role in the prayer process. Lastly, he asked, "Are there bowls in heaven that our prayers are stored in? If yes, how long does it take to fill the bowl with prayers before we can expect an answered from God? Are there angels with golden incense burners standing before the throne of God, waiting to collect our prayers, store it in bottles, and then mix it with incense before presenting it to God?

These were some of the questions I received that made me to develop a prayer training program, an intensive course on the art of prayer that helps to kick-start people's prayer life and make it very effective. It is a program used for teaching people the "how-to" and the "know-how" of prayer in seminars, conferences, summits, and prayer schools, so that they can cultivate a consistent prayer life. Knowing how prayer works and the different dynamics that enhance the effectiveness of our prayers is vital to consistent prayer.

MECHANISM OF PRAYER

The scenario in Revelation 8:1-6 shows the faithfulness of God to his word and principles. Just as I have mentioned before, heaven can't act on earth without the cooperation, authorization, or involvement of mankind. The passage talks about when the Lamb opened the seventh seal of God. There was silence in heaven for about half an hour because judgment was about to be poured out on the earth. The seven angels who stand before God were given trumpets to sound so the earth could be judged.

Since earth is man's domain, the angels who were to sound the trumpet waited until prayers were lifted by the saints, which an angel mixed with much incense and offered it as an offering on the gold altar to God before filling the censer with fire from the altar and throwing it on the earth, and there were voices, thunder, lightning, and earthquakes. It was after this that the seven angels with the trumpets started blowing them.

When we pray, the prayer does not go into any bottle or bowls; neither is there an angel waiting to catch our prayers and store it in a bowl. Psalm 103:20 declares that angels are mighty ones who carry out the word of God, obeying the voice of his word. The Cherubim, Mary the mother of our Lord Jesus, and the twenty-four elders in the courtroom of heaven do not interfere with our prayers. In fact, we don't need their assistance for our prayers to be heard and answered.

The Bible encourages us to address prayers to our heavenly Father, in the name of Jesus, by the help of the Holy Spirit who teaches us the word of God and helps us to pray in accordance with the will of the Father.

UNDERSTANDING the Art of Prayer (Revisited)

The word of God is the written revealed mind and counsel of God concerning humanity. Psalm 18:2 says that God has exalted his word above everything else. The Bible is the written word of God that contains the biblical truths, concepts, and principles that give us advantages in prayer. It also produces the faith we need to please God and obtain things from him.

Hebrews 11:6 says without faith, it is impossible to please God, because anyone who comes to him must believe that he lives and that he rewards those who earnestly seek him. James 1:6 declares that when you ask, you must believe and not doubt, because he who doubts is like a wave of the sea, blown and tossed by the wind. Romans 10:17 informs us that faith comes from hearing the word of God. And it is the Holy Spirit who teaches us the word of God and helps us to decode biblical truths, concepts, and principles from the word of God that we need to understand the ways and mind of the Father.

In conclusion, we pray to the Father, in the name of Jesus his Son, by the help of the Holy Spirit, in accordance with the written word of God that produces the faith we need to obtain things from the Father. Hebrews 4:16 encourages us to approach the throne of grace with confidence so that we may obtain mercy and find grace to help us in times of need. The finished work of Christ on the cross gives us access to the throne of heaven.

We don't need anybody's assistance for our prayers to be heard and answered by God once it is offered in the name of Jesus. Angels are God's ministers that perform his command. God is not a prayer collector but a prayer-answering God. He doesn't store prayers in any bottle or bowls in heaven.

MECHANISM OF PRAYER

The fact you didn't receive answers to your prayer does not mean he is storing them somewhere and waiting until the cup gets filled up before he respond. Since prayer gives heaven the permission to act on earth, the request you make today can become a legal ground for God to intervene in the future. Besides, God does things according to his own time, not your calendar. He uses the prayer you make now to act whenever he chooses to work in your life.

Therefore confess your sins to one another, and pray for one another, that you may be healed. The prayer of a righteous man has great power in its effects. Eli'jah was a man of like nature with ourselves and he prayed fervently that it might not rain, and for three years and six months it did not rain on the earth. Then he prayed again and the heaven gave rain, and the earth brought forth its fruit. (Jas. 5:16-18 RSV)

CHAPTER 7

KEYS TO EFFECTIVE PRAYER

As I mentioned earlier, prayer is a lifestyle. And to build a consistent prayer life, you have to learn the discipline of prayer. As a child of God, prayer is one of the spiritual exercises we do regularly to maintain our walk with the Holy Spirit. The degree to which you discipline yourself determines how consistent your prayer will be. It is very important to know the things that enhance the success of your prayer life so that you can use them to reinforce the consistency of your prayers. There are many things that determine the consistency of our prayer, though for the benefit of this subject, let's take a closer look at the following:

RELATIONSHIP WITH GOD

We notice in Jesus' pattern for prayer that it all begins with knowing who God is, knowing where he is, and accepting him as father. To say, "Our Father in heaven," means that prayer starts with a relationship with the Godhead.

UNDERSTANDING the Art of Prayer (Revisited)

You cannot cultivate a consistent prayer life without a good relationship with God, and to have a relationship with the Lord, there are things you have to do, according to scriptures.

The Bible declares in 2 Chronicles 7:14, "If my people who are called by my name will humble themselves, and pray, and seek my face, and turn from their wicked ways, I will hear from heaven and will forgive their sins, and heal their land." According to this passage, you have to be God's child before anything else (i.e. if my people who are called by my name), which means that relationship is the first key to consistent prayer.

To build a relationship with God, you have to be born again. To do that, you must acknowledge the great work he did for humanity by sending his only begotten Son, Jesus of Nazareth, to die for the sins of mankind. Then, you accept Christ's atoning sacrifice for the salvation of your soul and confess him as Lord, for with the heart one believes and is justified, and with the mouth one confesses and is saved (Rom. 10:9-10, Acts 4:12).

When you believe in your heart that Christ died and rose from the dead for the sins of humankind, you will be justified by the Father who forgives your sins and imputes his righteousness, which is by faith, to you so that you can have peace with God in Christ. Now, when you confess that Jesus is Lord, the eternal life of the Father will be infused into your spirit in Christ Jesus. This is done through the ministry of the Holy Spirit to regenerate your spirit from the spiritual death that came on humanity in the beginning through the sin of Adam.

This spiritual phenomenon is called *new birt*h or the *baptism by one Spirit* into the one body of Christ — the church. (For more information on this, please go to my book *The Oneness of God*, under the heading the "Divine Sonship of a Christian").

Once you are born again, you begin a new life with God in Christ. The Bible says that God so loved the world he gave his only Son, that whoever believes in him should not perish but have eternal life. God did not send his Son into the world to condemn it, but to save it through him (Jn.3:16-17). Salvation is found in no one else, for there is no other name given to men by which we must be saved than the name of Jesus, the Son of the living God (Acts 4:12). New birth, which commences a healthy relationship with the Godhead, is the first key to consistent prayer.

HUMILITY

The second key is humility. James 4:6 says God resists the proud but gives grace to the humble. Verse 4 declares that friendship with the world makes you an enemy of God, for anyone who chooses to be a friend of the world makes himself an enemy of God. Pride is a killer disease that everyone who desires a consistent prayer life must avoid by all means.

The apostle John also writes in his epistle that we shouldn't love the world or the things in it, because the things that the world offers — which are the lust of the flesh, the lust of the eyes, and the pride of life — do not come from the Father (1 Jn.2:15-16). When pride enters a person, it turns you against God and makes him your enemy.

UNDERSTANDING the Art of Prayer (Revisited)

And when God becomes your enemy, you can never succeed in prayer, because he won't listen to your cry for help. In fact, he resists the proud but gives grace to the humble.

Likewise you that are younger be subject to the elders. Clothe yourselves, all of you, with humility toward one another, for "God opposes the proud, but gives grace to the humble." Humble yourselves therefore under the mighty hand of God, that in due time he may exalt you.
(1 Pet.5:5-6 RSV).

Remember, prayer is a lifestyle that reflects the nature of the one you pray to. Pride is neither in God nor from him, but from the world. Two cannot walk together unless they are in agreement. For you to call and God to answer, you must remove anything in your life that the world you are living in has made a part of you, which may cause the Lord to turn his back on you. Pride is one of those things.

A proud person believes he has it all together. He is self-sufficient and independent. He neither regards God nor men. He is full of himself and arrogant. If he prays at all, he does it with pride. The Lord Jesus spoke a parable about two men who went to the temple to pray; one was a Pharisee and the other a tax collector.

The Pharisee lifted up his voice in prayer and said, "I thank you, God, that I am not like other people who cheat, rob, do evil, commit adultery, etc. or even like this tax collector. I fast twice a week and give a tenth of all that I get." But the tax collector stood at a distance and would not even lift up his eyes to heaven as he prayed. He said, "Be merciful to me, oh God, for I am a sinner."

KEYS TO EFFECTIVE PRAYER

The tax collector, who was seen as the sinner, went home justified before God rather than the Pharisee. Those who exalt themselves will be humbled, while those who humble themselves will be exalted, says the Lord. To be consistent in prayer, you must remain humble.

KNOWLEDGE

The third key I would like to talk about is knowledge. As I said earlier, knowledge is very important when building an active prayer life because what you know about prayer determines your attitudes toward prayer. Those who know much about prayer do incredible things with it. To be very effective in prayer, you have to read and learn about it.

When the disciples of Jesus noticed how their master prayed and the kind of results he produced, they realized there was something he knew about it that none of them knew that made him so consistent in prayer. So they asked him to teach them what he knew about prayer. Learn what prayer is, how to pray, why we pray, when to pray, where to pray, what to pray about, levels of prayer, power of prayer, types of prayer, laws and principles of prayer etc.

First, the fact John the Baptist and the Lord Jesus taught their disciples how to pray is an indication that prayer should be taught (Lk.11:1-4). Second, what you know about prayer must not die with you; it should be passed on to the next generation. Third, the knowledge people receive about prayer could change their prayer life. Fourth, those around us can learn the discipline of prayer from the way we live our lives.

Fifth, you can improve your prayer life by learning new techniques that work and by practicing them. Sixth, what you know determines your attitude toward prayer. Seventh, your level of effectiveness in prayer is proportional to the measure of revelation knowledge that you have about it.

The main difference between someone who spends months praying about an issue and another person who prays about the same thing and obtains it within hours is revelation knowledge. What you know determines your actions and words. Knowledge is very important to effective and consistent prayer. When you learn about prayer and practice what you know in accordance with the word of God, you will produce results.

To acquire right knowledge about prayer, join a prayer group and be committed, read good books on prayer, listen to CDs/DVDs, watch TV programs, attend prayer seminars, conferences, and conventions, ask questions on prayer related subjects, share what you learn with others, and develop a consistent prayer habit.

PRAISE AND WORSHIP

Praise and worship is one facet of prayer that everyone who desires a consistent prayer lifestyle must learn, because prayer is an act of worship. We praise God for what he does and worship him for who he is. Every true man and woman of prayer is a worshiper.

Jesus pattern for kingdom prayer begins with an act of worship, "Our Father in heaven, hallowed be your name." Prayer, praise, and worship are inseparable.

KEYS TO EFFECTIVE PRAYER

No one can pray effectively unless he is a true worshiper. We pray because we know God exists and that he hears and answers prayer. Psalm 22:3 says God is enthroned on the praises of his people.

Prayer authorizes God to interfere in human affairs, worship brings him down, while praise moves his hand. The three are interwoven. John 4:23-24 says a time is coming and it has now come when the true worshipers will worship the Father in spirit and in truth, for the Father seeks such people to worship him. The reason is that God is Spirit, and his worshipers must worship him in spirit and in truth. The Samaritans of Jesus' time worshiped what they didn't know, but the Jews knew who they worshiped. We pray because we know the God to whom we pray, and our commitment to him sets us apart from others.

After this the Moabites and Ammonites, and with them some of the Meunites, came against Jehoshaphat for battle. Some men came and told Jehoshaphat, "A great multitude is coming against you from Edom, from beyond the sea; and, behold, they are in Hazazon-tamar" (that is, Engedi). Then Jehoshaphat was afraid and set his face to seek the Lord, and proclaimed a fast throughout all Judah. And Judah assembled to seek help from the Lord; from all the cities of Judah they came to seek the Lord.
(2 Ch.20:1-4 ESV)

The passage above describes what King Jehoshaphat did when a vast army came against him for battle. He assembled all Judah to seek help from the Lord and proclaimed a fast. As the people gathered in the presence of God for fear of the great multitude, Jehoshaphat lifted up his voice in prayer and cried to the Lord for help.

UNDERSTANDING the Art of Prayer (Revisited)

"O our God, will you not judge them? For we have no power to face this vast army that is attacking us. We do not know what to do, but our eyes are upon you."

Then the Spirit of the Lord came upon Jahaziel son of Zechariah as he stood among the people, and he said, "Listen, King Jehoshaphat, and all who live in Judah and Jerusalem! This is what the Lord says to you: 'Do not be afraid or discouraged because of this vast army. For the battle is not yours, but God's."

As soon as King Jehoshaphat heard the word of prophecy, he encouraged his people to believe the Lord God and also to have faith in his prophet. After this, he took counsel with the people and appointed singers to march ahead of the army and sing praises to God, blessing his holy name. As they began to sing and bless the name of the Lord, God set an ambush against their enemies and caused them to start fighting among themselves. The Ammonites and Moabites turned against their allies from Mount Seir and killed every one of them. After they had completely destroyed the men from Seir, they started attacking and killing each other.

When King Jehoshaphat and his army arrived at the place, they saw only dead bodies lying on the ground, for their enemies turned against each other and helped to kill one another. None of them escaped. The Israelites found so more valuables among their enemies than they could carry. The plunder was so much that it took them three days to collect it all. They returned with great joy to Jerusalem because the Lord caused them to rejoice over their enemies.

KEYS TO EFFECTIVE PRAYER

When King Jehoshaphat heard about the sudden invasion of his land by his enemies, he was so afraid that he proclaimed a fast throughout his kingdom to seek God's intervention. As soon as the prophet gave him a prophetic direction, he resorted to praising and worshiping God. This gave him complete victory over the vast enemies that came against him for battle. His fasting and prayer, obedience to prophetic direction, praise, and worship gave him the victory which no other means could have given him (2 Ch.20:1-30). Make praising and worshiping God a habit and it will positively impact your prayer life.

PASSION

You are passionate about whatever you love. Passion is like a flame that burns in your heart. It drives you on, keeps you awake, pushes you into action, and causes you to do the things others consider very difficult or impossible.

Your passion for prayer determines what you do with your prayer life. Those who are passionate about prayer go the extra mile in building a consistent prayer life. They put in the time, energy, resources, and so on to make their prayer life effective. Unless you are passionate about prayer, you cannot be consistent.

Cambridge Advanced Learner's Dictionary defines a passion for something as, "An extreme interest in or wish for doing something, such as a hobby, activity, etc." Passion for prayer is an extreme interest in prayer — an interest that could make you give up anything for an opportunity to pray, talk, learn, or teach about prayer, attend prayer meetings, summits, seminars, conferences, and so on.

UNDERSTANDING the Art of Prayer (Revisited)

The story of the prophet Daniel will help to illustrate this point. The Bible says Daniel was one of the three administrators the King Darius appointed to supervise the one hundred and twenty officers he put in charge of the 120 provinces into which he divided his kingdom.

Daniel distinguished himself among the administrators in the way he handled government affairs and by his outstanding qualities, so that the king planned to set him over the whole kingdom. For this reason, the administrators and satraps started looking for grounds to bring charges against him in the way he was handling government affairs, but they could not find any fault with him, because he was faithful in the way he did his work.

At last they said to one another, "We will never find any basis for charges against this man Daniel unless it has something to do with the law of his God." So they went as a group to the king and said, "O King Darius, live forever! The royal administrators, prefects, satraps, advisers and governors have all agreed that the king should issue an edict and enforce the decree that anyone who prays to any god or man during the next thirty days, except to you, O king, shall be thrown into the lions' den. Now O king, issue the decree and put it in writing so that it cannot be altered – in accordance with the law of the Medes and Persians, which cannot be repealed." So King Darius put the decree in writing.

When Daniel learned that the decree had been signed, he went home and knelt down as usual in his upstairs room, with its windows opened toward Jerusalem. He prayed three times a day, just as he had always done, giving thanks to his God.

KEYS TO EFFECTIVE PRAYER

This is what passion for prayer will make you do. It will make you do things that others consider abnormal and irrational.

Daniel knew that praying to the most high God would cost him his freedom, career, life, etc. Still, he went ahead and prayed, because he knew what God is capable of doing when you completely depend on him and seek him with all your heart.

When the men who had been searching for grounds to accuse him found him praying and asking God for help, they went to the king and reminded him of his decree — that anyone who prayed to any god or man except to the king within thirty days would be thrown into the lion's den. The king, not knowing what had happened, said, "The thing stands fast, according to the law of the Medes and Persians, which cannot be revoked."

Then they told the king that Daniel, who was from Judah, did not respect the king or his decree, because he still prayed to his God three times a day. When the king heard the matter, he was greatly distressed and he looked for way to rescue Daniel. He made every effort until the sun went down, but he could not deliver Daniel from being thrown into the lions' den. Although the king couldn't save Daniel from being thrown into the lions' den, Daniel's God sent his angel to shut the mouths of the lions so that they would not hurt him in the den (Dan.6:1-24).

Passion for prayer will make you do things others consider unwise, just like the prophet Daniel, who was ready to lose everything to maintain his relationship and prayers to God. Even when he learned that praying to God would send him to the lions' den, he couldn't help praying three times because of his love and commitment to God.

His passion for prayer helped him to stay focused and steady at a time when everything turned against him and prayer became impossible. There will always be times when things fall apart and prayer becomes unthinkable, and at such times, it's only the passion you have for prayer that will make you to pray.

FELLOWSHIP

Proverbs 27:17 says that as iron sharpens iron, so one person sharpens another. There is no better way to make prayer a habit and to learn new techniques of prayer than by being where it is done and hanging out with those who pray regularly.

One of the easiest ways to do this is to join a prayer meeting and to be committed. Another way is by attending prayer seminars, conferences, conventions, and the like. Look for those who are as passionate about prayer as you are, and share your experiences with each other.

Acts 4:13 declares that when the members of the Sanhedrin saw the boldness of Peter and John, they were amazed, because they realized the two men had no special training in the scriptures. So they acknowledged it was because Peter and John had been with Jesus that they could speak the way they did. Being around the Lord Jesus changed their whole lives. This is what happens when you fellowship with those who are effective and consistent in prayer: their lifestyle will impart and change your attitude toward prayer.

The Bible talks about how Barnabas went to Tarsus to look for Saul and brought him to Antioch. Both of them stayed there with the church for a whole year and taught many people.

KEYS TO EFFECTIVE PRAYER

In the end, the believers were first called Christians at Antioch, because they were changed and transformed to the image of Christ, so that others look at them and said they were like Christ.

Then Barnabas went to Tarsus to look for Saul, and when he found him, he brought him to Antioch. So for a whole year Barnabas and Saul met with the church and taught great numbers of people. The disciples were called Christians first at Antioch.
(Acts 11:25-26 NIV)

To be consistent in prayer, hang out with people who understand the art of prayer, who value it, talk about it, and pray regularly. Whatever you do on a regular basis over a period of time becomes a habit, and when a habit is sustained, it becomes a character. If you have the habit of willingly praying with others on regular basis and you maintain it, it will automatically become a way of life. And the best and easiest way to do it is through fellowship.

Exodus 34:28-33 talks about how Moses went up to Mount Sinai and remained in the presence of God for forty days and nights without food or water to receive the Ten Commandments. While on the mountain communing with the Lord, he didn't realize something had changed in him. When he finally came down to the people, the passage declares that Moses' face was radiant, because the glory of God rubbed off on him while he tarried in God's presence and talked with him. The amazing thing about the story is that Moses didn't know that his face shone and reflected the glory of God until those in the camp saw him and were scared to go near him.

When you fellowship with those who are prayerful and who consistently attend prayer meetings, what they have and what they do will start rubbing off on you automatically. Look for a good prayer ministry or fellowship, and join them to learn how they pray. Stay connected and committed to the fellowship, and you will soon become like one of those you highly admire.

DETERMINATION

The very reason the prophet Daniel was able to stand and pray three times with his windows opened toward Jerusalem as he had always done is that he made up his mind to do it, regardless of the king's edict. He was determined to remain consistent in his prayer, despite the threat and danger of being thrown into the lions' den in accordance with the king's decree.

Determination is the willpower, firmness of purpose, and strength of mind and character that enables you to keep at something no matter how difficult it may be. Unless you stand for something, you will fall for anything. And unless you are determine to maintain a consistent prayer life, many things will come your way to hinder you from praying the way you ought to.

Prayer is a lifestyle, not just a religious activity. And to be consistent in prayer, you have to learn the discipline and do it like you mean it. Prayer is hard work, and unless you are determined to pray, you can't do it on regular basis. The weakness of one's body could become the main hindrance to consistent prayer unless we learn to discipline ourselves.

Matthew 26:36-46 recounts how the Lord Jesus took Peter, James, and John with him to Gethsemane to pray.

KEYS TO EFFECTIVE PRAYER

The passage says that he was sorrowful and troubled, and he said to his disciples that his soul was overwhelmed with sorrow to the point of death. So, he asked them to keep watch with him as he went a little farther to pray.

When he came back, he found them sleeping. "Could you not watch with me for one hour?" he asked Peter. He noticed that they were willing to pray, but the weakness of the flesh hindered them from doing so. Therefore, he said, "Watch and pray so that you may not enter into temptation. The spirit is willing, but the flesh is weak." He went away the second time to pray and when he returned, he found them sleeping again because their eyes were heavy. He did the same thing a third time, and when he returned, he found them still sleeping.

Like Peter, James, and John — who could not stand in prayer for one hour when the Lord Jesus took them with him to Gethsemane to keep watch in prayer because of the weight of the atoning sacrifice that he needed to make for human souls, which troubled his heart and overwhelmed him to the point of death — many of us sleep when we are supposed to pray. To be effective and consistent in prayer, we must be determined to pay the necessary price.

This reminds me of the three Hebrew boys who King Nebuchadnezzar took to Babylon from Judah. One day, the king made an image of gold and sent messages to the satraps, prefects, governors, advisers, treasurers, judges, magistrates, and all the provincial officials to come to the dedication of the image he had set up.

UNDERSTANDING the Art of Prayer (Revisited)

When they arrived, they all stood in front of the image to worship it, because King Nebuchadnezzar commanded that at the sound of the horn, flute, zither, lyre, harp, pipes, and other musical instruments, everyone was to bow to the ground and worship the golden image, and whoever did not worship it would be thrown into a blazing furnace.

As soon as the people heard the sound of the musical instruments, they all fell down and worshiped the golden image. But Shadrach, Meshach, and Abednego did not obey the king's command to worship the image. Some people denounced them to the king and told him that there were some Jews whom the king had appointed over the affairs of the province of Babylon who weren't paying attention the king, serving his god, or worshiping the golden image he had commanded everyone to worship.

When the king heard that, he was furious and he ordered that Shadrach, Meshach, and Abednego be brought before him. "Is it true Shadrach, Meshach, and Abednego, that you refuse to serve my gods or worship the golden image I have set up?" Nebuchadnezzar asked them. "If you are ready when you hear the sound of the musical instruments to worship the image I have made, very good. But if you do not worship, you will be thrown immediately into a blazing furnace. What god will be able to rescue you from my hand?"

Shadrach, Meshach, and Abednego replied the king, "O Nebuchadnezzar, we have no need to answer you in this matter. If this be so, our God whom we serve is able to deliver us from the burning fiery furnace, and he will deliver us out of your hand, O king.

But if not, be it known to you, O king, that we will not serve your gods or worship the golden image that you have set up."

For this reason, the king was very angry with them, and his attitude toward them changed. He ordered that the furnace be heated seven times hotter than usual before commanding some of the strongest soldiers in his army to tie up Shadrach, Meshach, and Abednego, and to throw them into the blazing furnace. Because the king's command was urgent and the furnace was overheated, the flames of the fire killed the soldiers as they threw the three men in.

The king jumped up in amazement and asked his advisers, "Did we not tie up three men and throw them into the fire?" "Certainly, your Majesty," they replied. He said to them, "I see four men unbound and unharmed walking around in the fire, and the fourth looks like the son of the gods." Then he approached the furnace and shouted, "Shadrach, Meshach, and Abednego, servants of the most high God, come out! Come here!"

When they came out of the fire, everyone crowded around them and noticed that their bodies were not harmed, their hair was not singed, their clothes were not burnt, and there was no smell of smoke on them (Dan.3:1-30).

At the end of the day, their determination to stand for what they believed in finally paid off. In verses 28 and 29, King Nebuchadnezzar said, "Praise be to the God of Shadrach, Meshach, and Abednego who has sent his angel and rescued his servants! They trusted in him and defied the king's command and were willing to give up their lives rather than serve or worship any god except their own God.

Therefore, I decree that the people of any nation or language who say anything against the God of Shadrach, Meshach, and Abednego be cut into pieces and their houses be turned into piles of rubble, for no other god can save in this way."

Then the king promoted them. God is faithful, and he will certainly reward those who diligently seek him day and night.

PRAYER LANGUAGE

Prayer language is the ability given by the Holy Spirit to God's people that enables us to say deep and hidden things that cannot be expressed in any known human language. Some call it "tongue talking" or "speaking in tongues" while others call it "praying in the Spirit". It is a spiritual phenomenon that usually occurs at the baptism with the Holy Spirit, which is accompanied with the initial sign of speaking in tongues.

It is a language that is exclusively reserved for prayer. This makes Christianity the only religion on earth that has a special language for prayer that no one can understand or interpret. It is not meant for buying or selling, but for communicating with God. The language is given to the body of Christ to secure our line and improve our communication with our father in heaven. It is a spiritual language that connects us to the spirit world (heaven). Since prayer is a private and personal thing, the prayer language allows us to put everyone else, including Satan out of our communication with God (Matt.6:6).

Other religions use human languages and dialects in prayers, but we Christians have a unique spiritual language that is solely for prayer.

KEYS TO EFFECTIVE PRAYER

A language that the Lord Jesus gives to his body – the church to enable us talk to him in private, since no body on earth understands it. When you pray in tongues, your line is secure!

However, there are many controversies about the subject among Christians. Some believe it is mandatory for all believers to speak in tongues, while others claim it no longer exists (this is known as the cessation theory). A few others believe it is a sign given to few individuals, while certain groups believe it is of the devil.

A person's position regarding speaking in tongues depends on the knowledge or teaching he has about the subject, which establishes his belief and determines his attitude as it relates to tongue speaking. If you hang out with those who believe in the cessation theory, or with those who believe it is special gift given to some people in the body of Christ, or with those who think it is of the devil, you will never speak in tongues. Knowledge is power! This is why the prophet Hosea says people are destroyed from lack of knowledge (Hos.4:6).

God gave man free will to choose whatever he wants, and he won't violate it. The Holy Spirit will not force a person to speak in tongues, either. When he comes on an individual, he normally expresses himself by enabling the person to speak in an unknown language. The Spirit comes, and then the tongues follow. Tongues enable you to articulate words in the Spirit to God. It is not meant for communicating among humans, but with God.

People always ask me whether it is possible for a person to be baptized with the Holy Spirit and not speak in tongues.

UNDERSTANDING the Art of Prayer (Revisited)

My response has always been this: God gave man the right of choice in the beginning. We have the choice to either let the Holy Spirit express himself freely or to silence him by resisting the urge he puts in our hearts when he comes on us.

Acts 7:51 talks about resisting the Holy Spirit, Ephesians 4:30 warns against grieving the Holy Spirit — by whom we have been sealed for the day of redemption — while 1 Thessalonians 5:19 says we should not quench the Holy Spirit. When people resist, oppose, or forbid the Holy Spirit from expressing himself through them, they grieve or sadden him, and if it continues, they will quench or completely silence him.

None can say Jesus is Lord without the help of the Holy Spirit, and it is the Holy Spirit who makes us one with the Lord in the spirit (1 Co.12:3, 6:17). Romans 8:9 says if anyone does not have the Spirit of Christ, he does not belong to him, for without the Holy Spirit, God's eternal life that brings us into oneness with the Godhead in Christ cannot be infused into our spirit at new birth for regeneration from spiritual death that came on humanity through the sin of Adam (for more information on this, please go to my book *The Oneness of God*).

This then implies that the fact someone doesn't speak in tongues does not mean they don't have him in their lives. There are stages in the manifestation of the Holy Spirit to every child of God (for more on this, please go to my book, *The Holy Spirit,* under the heading "The Holy Ghost and man.) The main reasons people silence the Holy Spirit includes the following:

KEYS TO EFFECTIVE PRAYER

First: the cessation theory, which asserts that spiritual gifts and speaking in tongues ceased with the twelve Apostles after the church was firmly established (1Co.13:8). They believe that since the completion of the canon of Scripture, tongues and other supernatural phenomenon that were evident in the primitive church ended.

Second: the belief that speaking in tongues is of the devil. Some believe that speaking in an unknown tongue is a diabolical practice, since they do not understand what they say.

Third: the belief that speaking in tongues is one of the gifts of the Holy Spirit that he gives to whoever he wills, which means that if a person doesn't speak, it is an indication that the Holy Spirit chooses not to give him the gift.

Fourth: misinterpretation of some Bible verses such as 1 Corinthians 14:13, which says that anyone who speaks in a tongue should pray that he may interpret what he says. They feel one must understand what he says before speaking in tongues. In verse 19 of the same chapter, Paul declares that he would rather speak five understandable words to help others than ten thousand words in an unknown tongue, while verse 23 says that if people who don't understand tongues come in your midst and hear everyone speaking in an unknown language, will they not think you are out of your mind?

We have to understand the difference between the gift of tongues and tongues as a sign. The Holy Spirit uses the first to unfold the mind of God to the people, and so it has to be interpreted in order that the people can understand what God is saying to the church.

UNDERSTANDING the Art of Prayer (Revisited)

It is used for prophesying or declaring the mind of God to the church in order to edify and give the people direction (to strengthen, encourage, and comfort the church).

But the second is used to convey the mind of the people to God, some deep secrets that none can understand except God. This is why it is called a prayer language, because it connects men to God. Prayers are not offered to humans but God, and the second tongue serves this purpose. Verse 2 declares that anyone who speaks in tongue does not speak to people but to God, for none understands him as he utters mysteries by the Spirit. The first is God to man (brings God's words to humans), while the second is man to God (conveys man's words to God in a coded language that only God understands).

For anyone who speaks in a tongue does not speak to men but to God. Indeed, no one understands him; he utters mysteries with his spirit. But everyone who prophesies speaks to men for their strengthening, encouragement and comfort. He who speaks in a tongue edifies himself, but he who prophesies edifies the church. I would like every one of you to speak in tongues, but I would rather have you prophesy. He who prophesies is greater than one who speaks in tongues, unless he interprets, so that the church may be edified. Now, brothers, if I come to you and speak in tongues, what good will I be to you, unless I bring you some revelation or knowledge or prophecy or word of instruction?
(1 Co.14:2-7 NIV)

Fifth: some doubt whether it is the Holy Spirit urging them to speak in an unknown tongue or their imagination. Unless you are clear about this, you may never speak in tongues. When the Holy Spirit is the one urging you, it burns and glows in your heart.

The Bible tells us what happened to the disciples when the Lord Jesus spoke with them on the road to Emmaus after his resurrection. They said their hearts burned within them while he talked with them on the road and opened their eyes to scripture, even though they could not recognize him until he broke bread and gave them to eat (Lk.24:30-32). When the people heard the message of Peter on the day of Pentecost, scripture says the word cut or pierced their heart (Acts 2:37). The word of God burns like fire and pierces the heart.

Sixth: some are just too concerned about what people might say if they speak in a new tongue. Shame is a killer disease! The Lord said in Luke 9:26 that whoever is ashamed of him and his word, he too will be ashamed of that person when he returns in his glory and in the glory of the Father and the holy angels. You have to take your eyes off what others think and stay focused on what God wants you to do in order to be effective in spiritual things.

Seventh: others are held captive and hindered from speaking because of fear of being mocked or ridiculed by others. The fear of the unknown has caused many not to speak no matter how they feel about it in their mind. King Saul lost the kingdom because he feared the people and obeyed their voice rather than following the instruction God gave him.

Saul answered Samuel, "I have sinned. I have transgressed the Lord's command and your words. Because I was afraid of the people, I obeyed them. Now therefore, please forgive my sin and return with me so I can worship the Lord." Samuel replied to Saul, "I will not return with you. Because you rejected the word of the Lord, the Lord has rejected you from being king over Israel."

UNDERSTANDING the Art of Prayer (Revisited)

When Samuel turned to go, Saul grabbed the hem of his robe, and it tore. Samuel said to him, "The Lord has torn the kingship of Israel away from you today and has given it to your neighbor who is better than you. Furthermore, the Eternal One of Israel does not lie or change His mind, for He is not man who changes his mind."
(1 Sam.15:24-29 HCSB)

Eighth: lack of true knowledge about speaking in tongues has been the main reason many don't speak. Ignorance is a killer disease! Matthew 22:29 says we make mistakes because we don't know the scripture or the power of God. Knowledge is very important. Faith comes through the knowledge you have about the written word of God. The knowledge you have about spiritual things determines your actions.

Ninth: the environment in which a person lives could also cause a person to silence the urge, because we share the views of those with whom we hang out. You cannot hang out with those who openly criticize and condemn speaking in tongues and expect to speak it one day.

Tenth: some people have made up their mind not to speak as a result of their belief system. Such people can never break out until the stronghold in their mind is demolished.

Something happened to me the very first time I spoke in tongues. It was in a church meeting, during Bible study. I had listened to the late Archbishop Benson Idahosa speaking in tongues on a TV program as he preached before I went to church. On my way, I started having a strong desire to speak in tongues just like the archbishop did when he was praying.

KEYS TO EFFECTIVE PRAYER

Suddenly, a passage I had read earlier in Mark 16:17 that says, "And these signs will accompany those who believe: in my name they will drive out demons; they will speak in new tongues" popped up in my mind. Having prayed for the Holy Spirit to baptize me, the urge to say something similar to what I heard on TV became very strong in my heart. I started comparing the new tongues promised in the Bible to what papa Idahosa was speaking.

When I finally got to church, the urge to speak grew stronger in my heart. I was so focused on the desire that I couldn't hear what the man of God was saying anymore, even though I was in the church. I heard myself saying Holy Spirit fill me. All of a sudden, I started screaming and speaking in tongues. My whole body shook violently as I leaped to my feet and continue to speak uncontrollably for some minutes before going down on my knees. When I came to myself, I noticed everyone in the service was looking at me. I was so ashamed that I felt like leaving the place.

The pastor called me out because it was a small church, spoke about what had happened to the congregation, and then encouraged me to maintain it by praying regularly in tongues before he prayed for me. I didn't wait for the service to end before leaving because I was so ashamed.

When you silence the Holy Spirit by refusing him the right to express himself through you in an unknown tongues, it limits your effectiveness in prayer. Ephesians 6:18 encourages us to pray in the Spirit on all occasions with all kinds of prayers and requests.

We only talk about what we know. There are things the human eyes don't see. The only way we can fully cover all grounds in prayer is by praying in the Spirit.

UNDERSTANDING the Art of Prayer (Revisited)

Using the language of the spirit in prayer enables you to offer all kinds of prayers and requests at all times. It takes you beyond the limits of human knowledge and words to a dimension where you can deal with several things at the same time.

The Bible declares in 1 Corinthians 14:2 that anyone who speaks in tongues does not talk to humans but to God, because no one understands him except God alone. True tongues is a coded heavenly language that Satan and his cohorts cannot decode. Verse 4 says he who speaks in tongue strengthens or edifies himself, while the one who prophesies edifies the entire church. Jude 20 also encourages us to build ourselves up in our most holy faith and praying in the Holy Spirit. Praying in tongues builds us up in Christ.

The apostle Paul declares in 1Corinthians 14:5 that he would like everyone to speak in tongues. At the same time, he would rather have them prophecy because the one who prophesies strengthens, encourages, and comforts the whole church. This is what makes the gift of tongues greater than the tongue that is for signs and prayer. In fact, the first is given to selected individuals as the Spirit wills (1 Co.12:7, 10-11), while the second is for everyone who desires and asks for it (Mk.16:17, Acts 2:4).

Romans 8:26-27 says that we do not know what we ought to pray for, but the Spirit helps us in our weakness by interceding for us with groaning that cannot be expressed in words. For those who refuse to speak in tongues, there is no way the Holy Spirit can help them in their weakness with groans that words cannot express. Verse 27 says the God who searches the heart knows the mind of the Spirit because he intercedes for us in accordance with the will of God. 1 John 5:14 declares that if we ask anything according to God's will, he hears us.

KEYS TO EFFECTIVE PRAYER

The Bible declares in 1Corinthians 2:10-11 that the Spirit searches the deep things of God, and that he also knows the mind of God. Those who don't speak in tongues depend on their knowledge and understanding in prayer. Using the language of the Spirit in prayer establishes us in God's will, and makes us very effective.

For if I pray in a tongue, my spirit prays but my mind is unfruitful. What am I to do? I will pray with my spirit, but I will pray with my mind also; I will sing praise with my spirit, but I will sing with my mind also. Otherwise, if you give thanks with your spirit, how can anyone in the position of an outsider say "Amen" to your thanksgiving when he does not know what you are saying? For you may be giving thanks well enough, but the other person is not being built up. I thank God that I speak in tongues more than all of you. Nevertheless, in church I would rather speak five words with my mind in order to instruct others, than ten thousand words in a tongue.
(1 Co.14:14-19 ESV)

The apostle Paul said in the above passage that he speaks in tongues more than all the people to whom he was addressing the letter at the time. Inasmuch as speaking in tongues is important, praying with understanding is also important. Paul says that when you speak in tongues, your spirit prays but your mind is unfruitful. So, he encourages us to pray and sing both in our spirit and mind.

To do this, use your mind or intelligence to establish legal grounds based on biblical truths, concepts, and principles from the written word of God on which you stand in prayer before taking it up to a higher dimension using the prayer language or tongues.

Switching between the mind and spirit should be spontaneous. For example, maybe you are praying for open heaven.

UNDERSTANDING the Art of Prayer (Revisited)

There are few things that provoke open heaven, and prayer is one of them. Luke 3:21b says as Jesus was praying, the heaven opened. Use the scripture to establish legal ground in Jesus name, and then command your heaven to open by divine authority before switching to the Spirit or praying in the Holy Ghost, and then back to your understanding or verse versa.

FAITH

Much has been said about faith because of its importance to effective and consistent prayer. Without faith, you cannot cultivate a consistent prayer life. Whoever prays to God must believe he lives, hears, and answers prayer. The degree of your faith determines the consistency of your prayer. To build your faith, you must exercise it. And to exercise your faith, you have to work it.

James 2:17 says that when faith is not accompanied by works, it is dead. It is one thing to say that prayer can heal a sick person, yet is another for you to go out there and pray for a sick person to be healed. Unless you put your faith to work, it has no life or power. The more you stretch your faith through prayer, the more it grows. But when it is dormant or inactive, it dies. The apostle James writes:

Is anyone among you suffering? Let him pray. Is anyone cheerful? Let him sing praise. Is anyone among you sick? Let him call for the elders of the church, and let them pray over him, anointing him with oil in the name of the Lord. And the prayer of faith will save the one who is sick, and the Lord will raise him up. And if he has committed sins, he will be forgiven.
(Jas. 5:13-15 ESV)

KEYS TO EFFECTIVE PRAYER

The passage above says that if anyone is suffering, afflicted, broken, distressed, in pain sorrow, grief, anguish, or misery, let him not complain, murmur, weep, hire a lawyer, go see doctor, talk to friends, kill himself, get depressed, frustrated, run away, or hide himself, but pray. The prayer of faith moves the hand of God and works wonders.

Romans 10:17 declares that faith comes by hearing the word of God. The more scripture you know and understand, the more revelation knowledge you'll have about God. And the more revelation knowledge you have about God, the more your faith increases. This is why 2 Peter 1:5 encourages us to do all we can to add to our faith, because faith grows. The more you exercise your faith in prayer, the more effective and consistent you become in prayer, and the more your faith increases.

When you pray for something by faith and God grants it, the answered prayer establishes your faith — gives you boldness, confidence, and authority in that area. Your faith in God and prayer makes you very effective and consistent. However, no matter how much faith you have about something, it has no value until you exercise it. The easiest way to exercise your faith and make it grow is prayer.

James 1:5 says that if anyone lacks wisdom, he should ask God, who gives to all without finding fault, and it will be given to him. In addition, verse 6 declares that he must ask in faith without doubting, because the one who doubts is like a wave of the sea that is driven and tossed by the wind. Verse 7 concludes that such a person should not expect to receive anything from God.

And He said to His disciples, "It is inevitable that stumbling blocks should come, but woe to him through whom they come! It would be better for him if a millstone were hung around his neck and he were thrown into the sea, than that he should cause one of these little ones to stumble. Be on your guard! If your brother sins, rebuke him; and if he repents, forgive him. And if he sins against you seven times a day, and returns to you seven times, saying, 'I repent,' forgive him." And the apostles said to the Lord, "Increase our faith!"
(Lk.17:1-5 NASB)

The above passage establishes the fact that faith can increase. If faith can be increased, it means it grows. When the disciples asked the Lord to increase their faith, he said, "If you have faith as small as the mustard seed, you could say to this mulberry tree, 'Be uprooted and planted in the sea,' and it would obey you." This means that the easiest way to increase our faith is by prayer. There is no way you can command a tree except by prayer. The same way faith makes your prayer effective and consistent, prayer activates and increases your faith.

GRATITUDE

Whenever God does something for us, the Bible encourages us to thank him. Thanksgiving is a higher dimension of prayer that produces the miraculous. The Bible tells us to enter God's gates with thanksgiving and his courts with praise. Be thankful to him and bless his name, says the psalmist (Ps.100:4). The power of thanksgiving opens the gates of heaven.

There is a passage in Luke 17:11-19 that I love so much because of the way it highlights the power of thanksgiving.

KEYS TO EFFECTIVE PRAYER

It talks about ten lepers who cried out in a loud voice to Jesus for mercy. They stood at a distance and could not come near him because of their health condition.

The Law of Moses made it unlawful for anyone with leprosy to come near those without the disease. They were to live in isolation and be separated from all that they had (Lev. 13:45-46). The sickness forced them out of their homes and took everything from them, including their identity, so that their names were not even mentioned.

When Jesus heard their cry for mercy, he gave them a prophetic direction by asking them to go show themselves to the priests. According to the Law, the priests had to examine them to see whether they had recovered from the deadly disease. This is something people do after they have been healed, but Jesus asked them to take the step of faith even though there was no sign of healing. Their obedience to the prophetic direction he gave them provoked the miracle.

People often miss their miracle because of lack of faith and disobedience to prophetic direction. It may not look like what you are praying for, but take the step of faith and do whatever you are asked to do once your spirit witness or convinces you. You will be glad you did.

On their way to go see the priest, one of them noticed that he had been healed. So he came back, praising God in a loud voice. The passage says that he threw himself at Jesus' feet and thanked him. The next sentence says that he was a Samaritan.

UNDERSTANDING the Art of Prayer (Revisited)

Before he came to thank God, he was lost in the situation in which he found himself, and no one knew his identity or origin, for leprosy had eaten it up. But the power of thanksgiving restored his identity and origin without him even asking for it.

In addition, Jesus asked, "Where not ten cleansed? Where are the nine?" This means that the man was set apart and distinguished from the other nine, even though he used to be at the same level with them. His act of gratitude separated him and set him apart from his associates. The power of thanksgiving sets you apart.

Third, Jesus said to him, "Rise!" Arise means to ascend, climb, go up, or increase. The sickness stagnated him and put his destiny on hold, but his gratitude lifted and caused him to rise.

Fourth, Jesus said to him, "Go your way!" The leprosy restricted his movement for a long time and placed an embargo on his destiny, but his thanksgiving lifted it and catapulted him to his destiny.

Fifth, Jesus said, "Your faith has made you well!" Some versions say whole or complete. This means fullness or completeness. Everything that concerns him was made perfect.

We notice in the above passage that his cry for help or mercy, which is a level of prayer, provoked a divine direction. However, his gratitude, which is a higher dimension of prayer, restored his identity, distinguished him, lifted him, broke the limitations in his way, and perfected all that concerned him. This is why the Bible declares in 1 Thessalonians 5:17-18 that we should pray without ceasing and give thanks in all circumstances, for this is God's will for us in Christ Jesus.

KEYS TO EFFECTIVE PRAYER

The will of God is not that we go through diverse circumstances, as some think, but that in whatever situation we are in, we have to give thanks, because the power of thanksgiving can turn things around. Thanksgiving is a higher form of prayer that produces the miraculous.

SACRIFICE

Merriam-Webster's Dictionary (2017 edition), include the following in its definition of sacrifice, "The act of giving up something that you want to keep especially in order to get or do something else or to help someone."

Sacrifice is something valuable, precious, costly, or important that you give up to make your prayer effective and consistent. This may include food, time, habits, money, relationships, investments, sleep, comfort, pleasure, and so on, for prayer. Prayer is an act of worship, and the place of prayer is a place of sacrifice.

A time will come when you have to give up certain things you treasure in order to maintain a consistent prayer life. This is one of the reasons prayer is hard work. It may sometimes cost you your beauty, if you have to abstain from food for a long time. Weight loss, tiredness, and unpleasant looks may be the first signs you will notice. Effective and consistent prayer will certainly cost you something. Your willingness to pay the price determines the kind of result your prayer produces.

Psalms 50:5 says gather to me my faithful people, who made a covenant with me by sacrifice.

UNDERSTANDING the Art of Prayer (Revisited)

This means that a true sacrifice carries, activates, and releases the power of covenant. The more sacrifice you make in prayer, the more effective your prayer becomes.

An altar has no power without a sacrifice, for sacrifice is the strength and voice of an altar. It takes sacrifices to strengthen your prayer altar. The Bible declares in Leviticus 6:12-13 that the fire on the altar must be kept burning; it must not go out. The priest was to add firewood to the fire every morning and burn the sacrifice on it. The more the sacrifice, the more the fire burns, and the more the fire burns, the more active the altar is. Likewise, the more sacrifice you make, the more intense and consistent your prayer becomes.

When some people pray and produce incredible results, others want to emulate them by merely learning how they pray, without seeking to find out what makes their prayer effective. Although it is a very good practice to imitate those who have produced positive results and done so many exploits through prayer, you also need to understand what they knew and did that gave them authority and made their prayer very effective.

Many crave consistent prayer but are not willing to make the necessary sacrifice that produces consistency in prayer. Consistency comes with a price! Those who produce consistent results in prayer always pay a certain price. The price you pay determines the weight and effectiveness of your prayer. Some Christians want their prayers to move the mountain and work wonders, yet are not ready to make the least sacrifice.

The Bible relates how a certain man brought his son to Jesus' disciples for deliverance, but they could not free the boy from the evil spirit.

KEYS TO EFFECTIVE PRAYER

When Jesus arrived at the place, he rebuked the demon and delivered the boy. The disciples of the Lord came to him in private and asked him why they could not cast the evil spirit out of the boy. "This kind does not go out except by prayer and fasting," Jesus said to them (Mk.9:28-29). When you make the necessary sacrifice that adds weight to your prayer, it strengthens and makes it more effective and powerful.

2 Kings 3:4-27 recounts how the prophet Elisha, a man with the double portion of his master Elijah's anointing, prophesied the victory of the king of Israel and his two allies when they attacked the king of Moab for rebelling against Joram, king of Israel. The passage shows how the Israelites invaded the Moabites, slaughtered them, destroyed their towns, stopped their springs, and cut down every good tree, according to the word of the man of God.

When the king of Moab saw that he was losing the battle, he took with him seven hundred swordsmen in an attempt to break through to the king of Edom, but they failed. Then he took his oldest son, who was to succeed him as king, and offered him as a sacrifice on the city wall.

Immediately, the power of his sacrifice turned the battle in his favor and forced the Israelites who were at the verge of victory to retreat and loose the battle. The king's oldest son was his most valuable asset — his heir and heritage (it is considered an abomination in some African culture for the crown prince to die before ascending the throne). Yet, he offered him as sacrifice to negate the power of Elisha's prophecy against him and his people.

UNDERSTANDING the Art of Prayer (Revisited)

The book of Esther 3:7 shows how Haman, son of Hammedatha the Agagite, used a whole year to consult an oracle for a favorable day to destroy the Jewish people. In verse 9, he offered to pay ten thousand talents of silver into the royal treasury for the destruction of God's people. According to the *Bible Knowledge Commentary*, "Ten thousand talents of silver weighed about 750,000 pounds, an enormous amount worth millions of dollars in present-day currency."[*] The power of sacrifice cannot be underestimated in determining the effectiveness and consistency of one's prayer.

Acts 23:12-14 tells how more than forty men formed a conspiracy and bound themselves with an oath not to eat or drink until they had killed Paul. They willingly gave up food and drink in an attempt to kill the apostle Paul. In addition, they went to the chief priests and elders to get everyone involved in their evil plot.

You have no idea how much sacrifice the wicked are willing to make, and how far they are prepared to go in order to destroy you. Balak son of Zippor, the king of Moab, built twenty-one altars and offered twenty-one bulls and twenty-one rams (forty-two in all) on the altars for Balaam son of Beor to place a curse on the Israelites (Num.23:1-30).

And Moab was exceedingly afraid of the people because they were many, and Moab was sick with dread because of the children of Israel.

---

* From Bible Knowledge Commentary/Old Testament Copyright © 1983, 2000 Cook Communications Ministries; Bible Knowledge Commentary/New Testament Copyright © 1983, 2000 Cook Communications Ministries. All rights reserved.

KEYS TO EFFECTIVE PRAYER

So Moab said to the elders of Midian, "Now this company will lick up everything around us, as an ox licks up the grass of the field." And Balak the son of Zippor was king of the Moabites at that time. Then he sent messengers to Balaam the son of Beor at Pethor, which is near the River in the land of the sons of his people, to call him, saying: "Look, a people has come from Egypt. See, they cover the face of the earth, and are settling next to me! Therefore please come at once, curse this people for me, for they are too mighty for me. Perhaps I shall be able to defeat them and drive them out of the land, for I know that he whom you bless is blessed, and he whom you curse is cursed."
(Num 22:3-6 NKJV)

Sacrifice is not a choice but a necessity as it relates to effectiveness and consistency in prayer. Sacrifice is the price that guarantees the prize. If you can pay the sacrificial price tagged to consistent prayer, you will receive the prize of effectiveness and consistency in prayer.

The Scripture talks about how Christ was to suffer many things before entering his glory. He had to fulfill all that Moses and the Prophets said concerning him before the Father gave him the glory that he promised (Lk.24:25-27). Before he wore the crown of glory, he first wore the crown of thorns.

Mark 15:16-20 describes how the Roman soldiers led him into the palace, dressed him in a purple robe, and twisted together a crown of thorns that they placed on his head. They struck him on the head with a reed and spit on him. After they had mocked him, they took off the purple robe and put his own clothes on him before leading him out to be crucified.

This was the sacrifice Jesus had to make to enter his glory. Yours could be fasting, night prayer (vigil), reading your Bible and other books on prayer, attending prayer meetings and programs, holiness, humility, fellowship, or giving. The bottom line is that there is a price to pay for effective prayer.

FASTING

In my book, *The Oneness of God*, I wrote about the life-changing encounter I had in 2003 that turned my life around. Before that day, I had given God the first hour of my day after a friend explained to me how his pastor asked him not to eat from 6 a.m. till 12 p.m. for some time.

As soon as I heard that, my spirit was so troubled that I couldn't stop thinking about it all day. Somebody else told me that same day that I needed to fast to move the hand of God in my favor. The whole thing troubled my heart because I didn't like fasting at all.

In a dream at night, someone walked up to me and handed me a video tape on which was written "The Life of Caesar", and asked me to watch the video. It was a documentary on all I was supposed to do to get to where I was destined to be in life. Fasting was one of the things the documentary said I was to do. As the person spoke about my life, he highlighted certain things I needed to do that helped me to become what I was destined to be. At the time, fasting was one of the things I always avoided, because I don't like to fast.

KEYS TO EFFECTIVE PRAYER

A couple of days later, I had another dream in which someone gave me a newspaper, and when I looked closely at the front page, it had my photo and an article written about all I did in life, the price I paid, the struggle and challenges I went through, and how my life ended. The church I went to was also teaching about fasting and prayer that I became so troubled and restless about it.

On the 8th of May, I decided to begin a fast by giving God the first six hours of my day (starting from 6 a.m. to 12 p.m.), because what my friend shared with me about the instruction his pastor gave him was so strong in my mind that I decided to do the same.

As soon as I started it, I had peace within. After about a week, I woke up one morning and completely forgot I was fasting until I had eaten breakfast. A few hours later, I had diarrhea and stomach pain that I will never forget. After the incident, I took the daily six hours of fasting very seriously.

From May 8, 2002 till October 23, 2003, I didn't eat breakfast. After the encounter I spoke about in my previous book, the Lord increased the number of hours I gave him daily from six to twelve, meaning I could not eat until 6 p.m. He explained to me that it was one of the things I had to do to get to fulfill my divine purpose. For the benefit of those who haven't read my former book, let me recount the experience here also.

"In 2003, I was in the house praying at about 11 p.m., when suddenly I heard one of the persons sleeping and snoring beside me calling my name and asking me to get closer. Initially, I did not understand what was going on until I heard my name about three times. He said "Caesar, get closer, for I am the Lord your God.

UNDERSTANDING the Art of Prayer (Revisited)

I have been seeking your attention, but you seem to be very busy with too many things, and this is why I have come to you this way — to show you deep and hidden things about Christ and the church."

When I heard that, I was a bit skeptical because I had never heard anyone say God appears to him or her in like manner. So I said to him, "If you are God, what is my mother's name?" I could have asked him some other question as a way of testing whether God was really the one speaking, but I believe the main reason I asked about my mother's name is that none of the people living with me in that house knew it.

We were about thirteen in number and I had not told any of them my mother's name because we all met at the place for the first time. Knowing also that God knows all things gave me the confidence to ask him something I knew the person didn't know about me. I said to myself, if God is the one talking through the person, he should know my mom's name.

In response to my question, he chuckled and said, "O Caesar," and then he kept quiet for a while before saying my mother's name. In addition, he told me deep things about my life and family that surprised me. In the course of our discussion that lasted about six hours, he did so many things that were naturally impossible and gave me several signs to prove he was the one speaking to me.

As one of the signs, he revealed a deep secret to me about the person he was speaking through and one other person, and asked me to tell them what he has told me.

KEYS TO EFFECTIVE PRAYER

Very early in the morning I went and spoke to them about it for confirmation. As I was speaking, both of them trembled with fear and wondered how I knew about their individual top secrets before I told them how the Lord revealed them to me.

Another surprise came when the people started asking me questions about the experience. They said, "We heard you talking throughout the night but we couldn't understand what you were saying; neither did we hear the voice of the person you were speaking to. Can you tell us what happened to you last night?" It was a big surprise to me because the voice of the person he spoke through was as loud and clear as mine. I could not figure out why they heard me talking for about six hours and none of them understood what I was saying or heard the voice of the other person even though some of them were lying beside me in the living room. Even those in the bedroom could hear me because the doors were opened.

It was a three-bedroom apartment, the inner room was for the boss and the other two were for us. The girls shared one room while the other one was for the boys. Since we were about thirteen in the house, some laid in the bedroom while others slept in the living room where I was praying. Throughout the night, none used the bathroom as they normally do. That was something I couldn't understand, because people wake several times to use the bathroom, except that night.

That night, the Lord showed me several things about my life. He also spoke deeply about things that relate to Christ and the church from the Scriptures with detailed explanation of each point.

UNDERSTANDING the Art of Prayer (Revisited)

After that encounter and other subsequent revelation I received, the burden to write a book and share with others the revelation knowledge God gave me became so heavy that I started gathering materials and outlining key points to research and meditate."

From October 23, 2003 till July 17, 2007, I did not eat before 6 p.m. each day except Sundays, when I eat after the church service, because our pastor told us in accordance with the Bible that it was unscriptural to go into God's presence and leave mourning (Neh.8:9-12, Ezek.46:9). So I break the fast on Sundays after the church service. The number of days I fasted was about one thousand three hundred and sixty days (1,360), that is three years, eight months and twenty-four days. When I stopped the fast, I returned to the first six hours that started May 8, 2002 and continued on that till March 3, 2014, making it eleven years and ten months.

While the fasting was on, I had another encounter in which the Lord instructed me to come up higher. It happened on August 4, 2006, when the Lord said something like, "I will take your daily food from you today and give you my table in exchange. I will meet you at my table at the going down of the sun." Beginning that day until January 19, 2007, which was about five months and fifteen days, my daily food was a measure of bread and grape juice, and I was allowed to take it only in the evening. Below is a sample of what my daily food for five months and fifteen days was like.

KEYS TO EFFECTIVE PRAYER

This reminds me of what the Bible says about the prophet Ezekiel, whom the Lord instructed to eat bread and drink water at a set time, by measure, for a period of time.

Now go and get some wheat, barley, beans, lentils, millet, and emmer wheat, and mix them together in a storage jar. Use them to make bread for yourself during the 390 days you will be lying on your side. Ration this out to yourself, eight ounces of food for each day, and eat it at set times. Then measure out a jar of water for each day, and drink it at set times.
(Ezek.4:9-11 NLT)

During the time I lived on the Lord's Table, the mystery of the table was unfolded to me. I'll share that in a different book am hoping to publish sometime later by his grace. I call it the Lord's Table, a table like no other, because of the mystery surrounding the body and blood of the Lord Jesus that he gave to the church through his table.

I have no intention of defining fasting or writing on the different types fasting we have, because much work has been done by others in that area. The few things I would like to add is that fasting add weights and values to your prayer. It makes it more effective and consistent.

UNDERSTANDING the Art of Prayer (Revisited)

It is one of the means or channels God gave to the church to generate more spiritual power to enforce changes in the earth. Fasting lifts you above nature to a dimension in the spirit realm where the impossible happens.

I remember the day I was so exhausted that I didn't want to continue the fast, I heard a voice saying, "Unless you abide, you won't make it." The journey was long, tough, and very hard. But he kept saying, "Though they are seeking your life to destroy it, they won't find you, because I have hidden you." Fasting is one of the hiding places of God, a refuge and fortress that the wicked cannot break in to harm you.

On one occasion, the Lord showed me something that looked like a transparent bottle, and in it was grain. The bottle was tightly sealed with a cap as a huge bird moved around it. The bird tried to break the bottle with its beak and eat up the grain, but it couldn't, even though it tried several times.

Someone standing by me in the vision said that as long as the grain remained in the bottle with its cap on, the bird could not eat it, no matter how much it tried. But if the bottle opens and the grain fell out, the bird would eat it up. Then he stared at me and said, "As long as you abide, you are safe. Though they could see you, they cannot touch you. And unless you abide, you will not make it."

This is not to say that everyone must fast as much as I did to fulfill their assignment. Everyone has his cross to carry. The Bible never asked us to carry another man's cross, but your own cross (Matt.16:24). This is one of the things I had to do to become what I was destined to be.

KEYS TO EFFECTIVE PRAYER

The reason I am sharing it is to encourage anyone walking the same path, and to let them know that if God called you to something, he will see you through.

That is not to say we have arrived, though — life is in stages (Phi.3:12-14). We learn from other people's experience and share ours to encourage one another. For the Bible declares in Proverbs 27:17 that as iron sharpens iron, so one person sharpens another. There is no better way to encourage others than through personal experiences and testimonies. If God has done it for one, he can do it for another.

But they also complain, "Why do we fast and you don't look our way? Why do we humble ourselves and you don't even notice?" Well, here's why: The bottom line on your "fast days" is profit. You drive your employees much too hard. You fast, but at the same time you bicker and fight. You fast, but you swing a mean fist. The kind of fasting you do won't get your prayers off the ground. Do you think this is the kind of fast day I'm after: a day to show off humility? To put on a pious long face and parade around solemnly in black? Do you call that fasting, a fast day that I, God, would like? This is the kind of fast day I'm after: to break the chains of injustice, get rid of exploitation in the workplace, free the oppressed, cancel debts.
(Is.58:3-6 THE MESSAGE)

The passage above elaborates on some of the things that fasting does. It also highlights certain things that make fasting ineffective. Finally, it shows that fasting goes beyond mainly abstaining from food, pleasure, and humbling oneself.

God spoke through the mouth of his servant, the prophet Isaiah, that fasting adds strength or force to our prayers and makes it powerful enough to break the chains of injustice, stop exploitation in the workplace, free the oppressed, and cancel debts. This means that through fasting and prayer, a person can destroy the chains of wickedness from people's lives, overturn the burden of fruitless labor, set the oppressed free, break demonic yokes, and stop satanic assault, because fasting and prayer lift you up spiritually to a dimension where you can exercise your divine authority.

However, things like hatred, unforgiveness, quarreling, anger, sin, etc. would cause your fasting to lose its power and force. Verse 4 says when your fasting ends in a certain way, it won't add anything to your prayer. For effective prayer, we have to fast for the right purpose and do it the right way to produce a positive result.

COMMITMENT

One more key I would like to briefly talk about is commitment, because of its importance in building and maintaining a consistent prayer life. Although there are many other keys that enhance consistency in prayer, I will end with this for now.

Commitment denotes devotion, dedication, engagement, faithfulness, steadfastness, persistence, and so on. Those who are committed to prayer go out of their way to do things that enhance their prayer life. They are willing to make sacrifices to maintain a consistent prayer life. Consistency demands a certain level of commitment.

A closer look at the life of the apostle Paul shows how he fully devoted himself to the cause he believed in.

KEYS TO EFFECTIVE PRAYER

The Bible declares that when he arrived in Caesarea, he stayed in the house of Philip the Evangelist. After some days, a prophet named Agabus came from Judea to where Paul was staying, took Paul's belt, and tied his hand and feet with it. Then he said, "The Holy Spirit says, 'This is how the Jewish leaders at Jerusalem will bind the man who owns this belt and will hand him over to the gentiles.'"

When the people in the house heard it, they all pleaded with Paul not to go to Jerusalem. But I love how the apostle Paul answered them. He said, "Why are you weeping and breaking my heart? I am ready not only to be bound, but also to die in Jerusalem for the name of the Lord Jesus." The passage says when they could not persuade him, they gave up and said, "Let the will of the Lord be done." After some days, he got ready and went to Jerusalem (Acts 21:7-15).

Before he became an apostle of Christ, scripture reveals how devoted Paul was to the purpose he served at the time. He persecuted the church and went from house to house to arrest and put many Christians in prison. In his zeal to destroy Christianity, he went to the chief priest and asked him for a letter to the synagogue in Damascus, so that if he found any Christian, whether man or woman, he might take them as prisoners to Jerusalem.

The Lord Jesus had to intervene. He arrested, transformed, empowered, and sent Paul to build what he was trying to destroy (Acts 8 and 9). As soon as Paul found his new purpose, he committed and devoted himself to it in such a way that he was prepared to die for the cause.

UNDERSTANDING the Art of Prayer (Revisited)

He recounts the price he had to pay to maintain his walk in Christ in 2 Corinthians 11:23-27: he was frequently imprisoned, severely flogged, always faced death, received thirty-nine lashes, was beaten three times with rods, once was stoned, suffered shipwrecked three times, endured sleepless nights, suffered hunger and thirst, and often went without food.

Just as it happened to the apostle Paul, many things will come your way to stop you from praying. The enemy will orchestrate a lot of things to hinder you from praying. There will be a time when prayer becomes impossible. The only thing that will make you stand is your devotion to prayer.

When you are devoted to something, you'll go out of your way to do it. Against all the odds, the prophet Daniel prayed three times a day just as he had always done (Dan.6:1-11). This he did because he was wholly devoted to God and to prayer. The wicked will do anything to hinder the consistency of your prayer. They will attack you with sickness, depression, anger, frustration, confusion, affliction, lack, tiredness, lost, pain, un-forgiveness, regret, rejection, delay, sin, etc. in order to stop you from praying. It takes commitment to maintain consistency in prayer.

CHAPTER 8

DYNAMICS OF PRAYER

The dynamics of prayer refers to the power of prayer that produces the miraculous when activated. To activate this wonder-working power of prayer, you must be effective and consistent in prayer (go to chapter seven for more information on keys to effective prayer).

The understanding you have about the miracle-working power of prayer determines what you do with prayer when going through negative circumstances. No matter the situation you are in, prayer can bring you out of it and turn things around for you.

The miracle-working power of prayer changes lives, destinies, and situations any time it is activated because its source is the heavenly throne room where all power and authority is derived. And because it comes from heaven, which is a higher dimension than the earth, it changes and controls everything that is on earth (Jn. 3:31).

When you effectively pray with proper understanding of the power of prayer, you do wonders and produce the miraculous.

UNDERSTANDING the Art of Prayer (Revisited)

The effect of the power of prayer has no limit or boundary; it breaks barriers, works wonders, touches heaven and earth, releases healing and deliverance. There is no limit as to what prayer can do.

When your place of honor, blessing, and glory becomes that of humiliation, pain, frustration, confusion, or loss, resort to prayer, for it has the ability to turn things around for your good.

Before the Lord Jesus went to Bethany, he said the sickness of Lazarus would not end in death but for the glory of God, that he (the Son of God) may be glorified through it. If he were just a mere prophet, he would have said, "Thus says the Lord, this sickness is not unto death, but for the glory of God, that the Son of God might be glorified through it." Since he is God, he simply said the sickness would bring him glory.

Knowing that he was going to Bethany to be glorified, he stayed where he was for two more days and did not hurry to the place. Whoever hears this would think that as soon as Jesus entered Bethany, he would be honored, because the place was designed for his lifting.

When he finally arrived, he found that Lazarus had already been in the tomb four days. Lazarus' sister Martha, who spent her time preparing all kinds of food for the Lord Jesus the last time he visited them (Lk.10:38-40), said to him, "If you had been here, my brother would not have died," meaning the reason her brother died is because Jesus didn't come when she sent for him.

Remember, the Lord came to Bethany to be glorified, but the very first thing he received was to be indirectly accused of killing Lazarus.

Martha put the responsibility of Lazarus' death on him and left him at the gate as she went to call her sister Mary.

I do not know the distance from the gate to their house, but Jesus did not move from where Martha left him until Mary came from the house to meet him. Verse thirty says he had not yet come into the village, but was still in the place where Martha met him.

When Mary saw him, she said exactly the same thing her sister Martha had said earlier to the Lord Jesus. It stands to reason that the whole family and their friends had concluded that Jesus was responsible for Lazarus death, because the crowd looked at him and said almost the same thing, "Could not he who opened the eyes of the blind, have kept this man from dying?"

To everyone, Jesus had the solution but decided not to help. In fact, Mary had seen many instances as she followed Jesus around in his ministry, where he spoke a word and the person was healed, as in the case of the centurion whose servant was sick but Jesus healed him by the power of the spoken word (Lk.7:1-10), and the Canaanite woman whose daughter was demon-possessed and he delivered her without going to their house (Matt.15:21-28). Let's assume the Lord had a busy schedule so that he could not make time to come — he could have spoken a word and Lazarus would live and not die.

The people may say, the Lord could have come and heal Lazarus, but he didn't. Second, he could have at least spoken the word and Lazarus would live and not die, but he didn't. They saw him do these for others on several occasion. So, they put the responsibility of Lazarus' death on him.

UNDERSTANDING the Art of Prayer (Revisited)

When the Lord saw Mary weeping and all the Jews who came with her weeping also, he himself started crying (Jn.11:35). He came to Bethany to be gloried and lifted, but all he received was contrary to what the Father planned for him. He was accused and ignored by those who should have honored and celebrated him. His place of honor became one of shame, accusation, humiliation, and weeping, so he resorted to crying like every man would do when things fall apart.

We cry about our marriages, children, career, finances, relationships, projects, health, city, nation, work place, and so on when we are supposed to pray. Having cried for a while, he realized that crying wouldn't help the situation, but prayer could. So, he resorted to prayer and turned things around. Through prayer, he enforced the will of the Father, brought Lazarus from death to life, and turned Bethany to a place of glory and lifting for his ministry (Jn.11:1-44).

The Lord promised in John 14:12 that whoever believes in him will do the very works he did, and even do greater than that. If he was able to bring a dead situation to life and change the place of frustration, confusion, shame, accusation, pain, loss, weeping and death to that of celebration, glory, lifting, honor, joy, testimony, deliverance, and salvation through the power of prayer, we can do the same.

The scriptures cannot be broken. Has your place of rest, honor, promotion, blessings, and celebration become that of instability, disgrace, pain, frustration, demotion, curses, weeping, and loss? Resort to prayer! Use it to enforce a change, and turn things around in your favor. Prayer works!

DYNAMICS OF PRAYER

The transfiguration of Christ is another good example of what prayer can do. It highlights the miracle-working power of prayer. The passage tells how the Lord took Peter, James, and John with him up to the mountain to pray. And as he was praying, the appearance of his face changed, and his clothes became dazzling white.

About eight days after Jesus said this, he took Peter, John and James with him and went up onto a mountain to pray. As he was praying, the appearance of his face changed, and his clothes became as bright as a flash of lightning. Two men, Moses and Elijah, appeared in glorious splendor, talking with Jesus. They spoke about his departure, which he was about to bring to fulfillment at Jerusalem. Peter and his companions were very sleepy, but when they became fully awake, they saw his glory and the two men standing with him. As the men were leaving Jesus, Peter said to him, "Master, it is good for us to be here. Let us put up three shelters — one for you, one for Moses and one for Elijah." (He did not know what he was saying.) While he was speaking, a cloud appeared and enveloped them, and they were afraid as they entered the cloud. A voice came from the cloud, saying, "This is my Son, whom I have chosen; listen to him."
(Lk.9:28-35NIV)

Note here that the transfiguration occurred when he was praying, according to the above passage. This means that the power of prayer can change anything. And if Jesus' prayer could change both his face and the clothes he was wearing, your prayer can change anything in your life that you want to change.

While the Lord Jesus was experiencing the change, Peter and the other apostles were all sleeping.

UNDERSTANDING the Art of Prayer (Revisited)

It stands to reason that if they had prayed like Jesus did, they would also have experienced the same miracle Jesus had, because he took them there for prayer, but instead of praying, they fell asleep.

The prayer was so powerful that it moved him from the dimension he was in to a higher one where Moses (who represents the law) and Elijah (who represents the prophets) appeared in glory and spoke with him about the ultimate price he was to pay for human souls.

Luke 24:44 says everything that is written about him in the Law of Moses, the Prophets, and the Psalms must be fulfilled. So they came to give him more details about the mission: the nature, manner, place, time, etc. While all these things were going on, Peter and the other apostles were sleeping, and when they woke up, they saw his glory and the two men standing with him. Perhaps, if they had prayed when Jesus was praying, they too would have had the same experience.

Jesus' prayer changed his face, clothes, moved him to a higher dimension where he manifested his glory, attracted the two major signs of his prophetic destiny, and gave him insight to the nature, manner, place, and the timing for the accomplishment of his mission on earth.

1 Samuel 1:1-20 tells the story about how Hannah the wife of Elkanah, whose womb the Lord closed so she could not have children, used the miracle-working power of prayer to unblock her womb and turn her situation around.

The passage relates how she went with her husband Elkanah and her rival Peninnah to Shiloh every year to worship and make sacrifices to the Lord.

DYNAMICS OF PRAYER

On the day Elkanah presented his sacrifice, he would give portions of the meat to Peninnah his wife and each of her children. But to Hannah, he would give double portion because he loved her, even though the Lord had closed her womb.

Peninnah took advantage of the fact Hannah could not bear children and provoked her until she wept and would not eat. This happened each time they went to the house of God at Shiloh.

One day, after they had finished eating and drinking, Hannah was deeply distressed and she wept bitterly before the Lord in prayer moving only her lips, but her voice was not heard.

Eli, the high priest who was sitting beside the entrance of the Tabernacle, observed her moving only her lips as she prayed in her heart, and he thought she was drunk. He said to her, "How long are you going to stay drunk? Put your wine away from you." But Hannah answered, "No, my lord, I am a woman who is deeply troubled. I have drunk neither wine nor strong drink, but have poured out my soul before the Lord. Don't think I am a wicked woman, for I have been praying out of great anguish and sorrow." Then Eli answered, "Go in peace and may the God of Israel grant the request you have asked of him."

Then she went, ate something, and her face was no longer sad. The whole family got up early the next morning and went to worship the Lord before returning to their home at Ramah.

God remembered her and in due time, she conceived and gave birth to a son who she named Samuel, saying, "I asked the Lord for him."

UNDERSTANDING the Art of Prayer (Revisited)

Her prayer caused the Lord to remember her, open her womb, give her children, silence the voice of her rival, and turn her life around for the better.

There are so many people in the Bible who used the miracle-working power of prayer to turn their situation around. The reason is that prayer changes lives, enlarges territory, moves the hand of God, produces wonders, rescues from death, breaks yokes, brings liberty, provokes angelic intervention, gives you power over your adversaries, thwarts evil plots, reduces the risk of death, and brings promotion. It also produces spiritual, physical, and emotional healing. Prayer is medicinal!

CHAPTER 9

WONDERS OF PRAYER

The good thing about prayer is that it works. It moves heaven and earth, and it is the only indestructible bridge that connects divinity and humanity. With the proper understanding of the art of prayer, we can work miracles through it. And since prayer moves the great hand that controls all things, it changes the course of things at any time.

The Bible has several examples of how the men of old used prayer to work wonders and do the impossible in their time. The passage in 1 Chronicles 4:9-10 beautifully illustrates this point, in that it shows how Jabez used it to turn his destiny around.

THE PRAYER OF JABEZ

Jabez was more honorable than his brothers; and his mother called his name Jabez, saying, "Because I bore him in pain." Jabez called upon the God of Israel, saying, "Oh that you would bless me and enlarge my border,

and that your hand might be with me, and that you would keep me from harm so that it might not bring me pain!" And God granted what he asked.
(1Ch. 4:9-11ESV)

Jabez was more honorable than his brothers, says the above passage, and his mother gave him the name because she bore him in pain. He called upon the God of Israel and pleaded with the Lord to bless him and enlarge his territory and that the hand of the Lord would be with him and keep him from harm so he would be free from pain. And God granted him his request. Had Jabez not prayed, he would not have moved the mighty hand that controls all circumstances. God responds to prayer, and he uses the prayer of saints to work wonders on earth. No prayer, no miracle.

The wonders of prayer consist of mind-blowing, unbelievable, and often difficult to imagine acts of prayer. It is the beauty and glory of this great weapon God gave to humanity, which has always been underestimated by many whether in the church or in the world.

The passage we read about Jabez says that he was more honorable than his brothers, but it remains silent on what gave him the superiority over his brothers. The sentence ends with the saying that his mother named him Jabez because she bore him in pain.

In the Bible, a name plays a very significant role in relation to the origin, birth, position, or even the destiny of a person. I believe the reason his mother looked at him and gave him the name Jabez, meaning one who causes pain or sorrow, is not just because of the pain she had when giving birth to him.

WONDERS OF PRAYER

Since Genesis 3:16, John 16:21, and other passages of the Bible reveal that women go through pain in child birth, I think the circumstances surrounding his birth were so bad that his mother had to name him after it as a souvenir.

The word translated "honorable" is the Hebrew word "Kabad" or "Kabed" and it matches the Strong's Number "H3513". It means to be heavy, weighty, grievous, hard, rich, honorable, glorious, burdensome, honored, etc.

The *Theological Wordbook of the Old Testament* says the basic meaning of the word is "to be heavy, weighty," a meaning that is only rarely used literally, the figurative (e.g. "heavy with sin") being more common. From this figurative usage, it is an easy step to the concept of a "weighty" person in society — someone who is honorable, impressive, and worthy of respect. This latter usage is prevalent in more than half the occurrences in the Bible.[*]

From this point of view, the word translated "honorable" is rarely used literally, but when used figuratively, it could mean to command respect or attention. This means that Jabez commanded more attention than all his brothers. However, the Bible does not mention the very reason he had more influence than his siblings, although many suggest he was more successful than everyone else in the family, and that his siblings submitted to him because of his wealth and fame.

---

* (From Theological Wordbook of the Old Testament. Copyright © 1980 by The Moody Bible Institute of Chicago. All rights reserved. Used by permission.)

UNDERSTANDING the Art of Prayer (Revisited)

According to *Strong's* definitions, the word could be used in either a good or a bad sense. When used in a negative sense, it could mean burdensome, severe, dull, etc. while in the positive sense, it means numerous, rich, honorable, and so on. Causatively, it means to make weighty in both senses.

With this in mind, I think it is important that we take a closer look at this very word from both sides in order to really understand what made Jabez more honorable than his brothers, why his mother called him "one who causes pain," and what made him cry out to God for help.

Merriam-Webster's Dictionary includes in its definition of the word "weighty" the following: having a lot of weight, very important and serious, having the power to influence the opinions of other people.

This means that Jabez could have commanded more attention than all his siblings either because he was rich, honorable, or had plenty (in the positive sense), or because he was burdensome, severe, or dull (in the negative sense).

There is a high possibility that his mother named him Jabez because the pain she had when she gave birth to him was far beyond the normal birth pain every woman experiences when delivering a child. Given that names play a significant role in the destiny of people, I think the circumstances surrounding his birth were so bad that the joy of having a male child born to the family could not take away her pains. John 16:21 says a woman suffers the pain of labor when her child is born, but she forgets the anguish for the joy that a child is born into the world.

WONDERS OF PRAYER

Perhaps his health condition was so serious that his mother looked at him and felt so much frustration, pain, and sorrow, that the joy of having her boy alive could not make her feel good, and so she named him Jabez, being mindful of how much pain he would cause the family.

Causatively, the Hebrew word "Kabad" means of much importance or having the power to influence the opinion of other people, whether in a good or a bad sense. That is to say that Jabez commanded more attention than his siblings because of his condition, which made others put his affairs above their own. If it were wealth, riches, or fame that gave him superiority of means over his siblings, as some say, I think the nature of his prayer would have been different.

Before we consider the nature of Jabez's prayer, I would like to tell a little story about a friend who has three children. One of his kids has a disability that causes everyone in the family to puts his interest above their own. He goes to a Special Needs School, has a special doctor and a maid, and enjoys a lot of privileges and attention that the other members of the family don't have. His interest comes before every other person's, and when he is not doing well, it affects everyone in the house more than when someone else is not feeling too well.

The cost of taking care of this one child a month is more than what is takes to feed all the other family members. Every time I think about this child's health condition and how it gave him superiority of means over his siblings, though he is not the eldest, it gives me a clear picture of Jabez situation. A closer look at the nature of Jabez's prayer could help us in understanding the true condition of his life.

NATURE OF JABEZ'S PRAYER

Now Jabez was more honorable than his brothers, and his mother called his name Jabez, saying, "Because I bore him in pain." And Jabez called on the God of Israel saying, "Oh, that You would bless me indeed, and enlarge my territory, that Your hand would be with me, and that You would keep me from evil, that I may not cause pain!" So God granted him what he requested.
(1Ch. 4:9-10 NKJV)

1. Oh that you would bless me indeed
2. Enlarge my territory
3. Let your hand be with me
4. That you would keep me from evil
5. That I may not cause pain

BLESS ME INDEED: The Hebrew word translated "Blessed" here is "Barak" meaning to bless, to kneel, etc. It has a Strong's Number "H1288". The *Theological Wordbook of the Old Testament* says, "To bless in the OT means 'to endue with power for success, prosperity, fecundity, longevity, etc.'"

I believe Jabez got to a point in his life when he realized that the only one who could change his situation was God. Let's not forget that this event took place at a time when natural strength was very important because of the nature of work they did. Disability of any kind put you at the mercy of others and made you irrelevant to both your family and nation (you couldn't go to war or cultivate the land, and others had to provide in order for you to survive).

Jabez called on the God of Israel, who does incredible things, to endow him with power for success, prosperity, fecundity, and longevity because of what he was going through.

WONDERS OF PRAYER

I know some may object to this point of view, stressing he prayed because of his love for God and his desire to build a city for the scribes to do their work (1 Ch. 2:55).

All I can say about this is that what Jabez asked God for was something far beyond riches or wealth. His condition had weakened him so much that he needed to be empowered to break out of the confinement and fulfill his destiny.

ENLARGE MY TERRITORY: The word translated "enlarge" is the Hebrew word "Rabah," and it matches the Strong's Number "H7235". It means to increase in whatever respect, to become great, many, much, numerous, etc. Jabez needed to break out of the confinement and stagnation he was in.

Whenever I look at my friend's son, I can feel how much he desires to be free and be able to do things like every other person around him. Sometimes he tries to move and do certain things by himself, regardless of the pains he goes through. Jabez couldn't have been in any way different that he made that prayer to God.

LET YOUR HAND BE WITH ME: The hand of God speaks of his power. To ask for the hand of God is to seek his protection. Psalm 127:1 says that unless the Lord builds the house, its builders labor in vain, and unless he watches over the city, the watchmen stand guard in vain.

Jabez probably heard of how God delivered the sons of Jacob from bondage and brought them out of Egypt by his mighty hand, and he desired to have such a hand rest on his life and free him from whatever situation he was in.

UNDERSTANDING the Art of Prayer (Revisited)

THAT YOU KEEP ME FROM EVIL: I believe Jabez was so vulnerable that he prayed for God to protect him from evil or from anything that could harm him. Some dictionaries define evil as something that causes harm, injury, or destruction. There could have been many things he feared that he had to seek God's protection from all kinds of evil.

THAT I MAY NOT CAUSE PAIN: This is the bottom line of his prayer to God. Being conscious of his condition and how much pain he was causing those around him, he cried out to God to change the situation, because it got to the point where he didn't want to take it anymore.

If you have ever been in a situation that makes you feel and think you are responsible for the pain other people are going through, you will understand how frustrating, disturbing, distressing, confusing, or difficult it is to handle the guilt, sorrow, pain, anguish, and grief you feel within. Nobody in his right mind would want to be the cause of other person's misery.

There are times in life when it seems as if your world has come to an end. The more you try to put things together, the more they fall apart, and the more you try to fix them, the worse they become. The best thing to do at this time is to turn to God in prayer, as Jabez did.

Whatever your family, friends, certificates, knowledge, contacts, and possessions cannot do for you, God can, and the best way to move his hand and cause him to act in your favor is through prayer. Prayer works magic — it produces the impossible, works miracles, changes lives, and moves the only hand that controls all things.

CHAPTER 10

THE PRAYER OF CORNELIUS

The salvation of Cornelius and his family members is no doubt the result of his persistent prayer and giving, as we observe in the passage in Acts 10:1-48. The angel of the Lord that came to him clearly said, "Your prayers and gifts to the poor have come up as memorial offering before God. Send men to Joppa and bring one who is called Peter."

When the apostle Peter came to his house and started preaching the good news, the Holy Spirit came on all who heard the message. As soon as this happened, Peter instructed them to be baptized in the name of Jesus Christ.

Before Cornelius had the angelic visitation that brought salvation to his house, he had a successful career in the military. He was a captain of a division consisting of about 100 persons in the Roman army. The passage states that he was a captain of the Italian Regiment, which means his band was composed of soldiers born in Italy. This was a way of distinguishing them from those born in other parts of the Roman provinces, since Rome enlisted soldiers from different parts of the empire.

UNDERSTANDING the Art of Prayer (Revisited)

For Cornelius to command such division means he was very successful, because this special band would claim preeminence over other division that was composed of soldiers from outside Italy.

Apart from the fact Cornelius was a successful captain in the Roman army, he was a Roman citizen. Since Rome governed the world at the time, he had superiority of means above his colleagues who were not Romans. To really understand the kind of rights and privileges Roman citizens enjoyed those days, let's take a quick look at the life of the apostle Paul, who was born a Roman citizen, and observe how he used his citizenship to get certain benefits.

Acts 16:35-40 describes how the magistrates commanded Paul and Silas to be stripped, severely beaten, and thrown into prison because they delivered a slave girl who had a spirit of divination by which she predicted the future and earned her master much money.

The jailer put them in the inner cell and fastened their feet in the stocks so they wouldn't escape. The following morning, the magistrates sent their officers to the jailer with the order, "Let those men go." When the jailer told Paul that the magistrates have asked him to release them, he said to the jailer, "They have beaten us publicly, uncondemned, being Romans and have thrown us into prison; and do they now thrown us out secretly? No! Let them come themselves and take us out."

The passage says when the magistrates heard that Paul and Silas were Roman citizens, they were afraid.

THE PRAYER OF CORNELIUS

So they came and apologized to them, escorted them from the prison, and begged them to leave the city.

Another example occurred in Acts 22:22-29, when the commander ordered that Paul be brought into the barracks and examined by scourging in order to find out why the crowd was shouting at him the way they were. As they stretched him out for the lashes, Paul said to the centurion standing there, "Is it lawful for you to flog a Roman citizen who hasn't been tried?"

When the centurion heard that, he went and asked the commander, "What are you doing? This man is a Roman citizen." So the commander went to ask Paul whether he was truly a Roman citizen. When Paul told him that he got his citizenship by birth, scripture tells us that those who were about to interrogate him withdrew immediately. And the commander himself was scared when he realized that Paul was a Roman citizen because he had bound him.

With these two accounts in mind, there is no doubt that being a Roman citizen in those days was very advantageous, since it gave people a lot of privileges, such as free access to places, special treatment, and benefits that many would have had to pay a huge amount to receive, as in the case of the commander in Acts 22:28.

The passage says that Cornelius and his whole family were devout and God-fearing. He gave alms generously to the needy and prayed continually to God. A person can only give what he has. For him to have given much alms to those in need shows he wasn't poor.

UNDERSTANDING the Art of Prayer (Revisited)

Despite the fact Cornelius had a great career in the military (successfully climbing the corporate leader to become the captain of elite band), was a Roman citizen, gave generously from the abundance he had, and had a God-fearing family, there was something none of all his achievements could give him, and that was "salvation".

This means that no matter how much you have, there are things that your education, degrees, career, social status, contacts, money, influence, intelligence, family, or friends cannot give you. Cornelius knew this fact, and so he turned to persistent prayer and the giving of arms to move the mighty hand that controls all things. As he persistently sought the face of God for the missing link, the Lord sent him an angel that gave him divine direction as to what to do about his situation.

As earlier said, one of the things prayer does is that it provokes divine intervention and direction. The angel said, "Your prayer and your alms to the poor have come up as a memorial before God. Now send to Joppa, and call for one Simon, whose surname is Peter. He is staying with Simon the tanner, whose house is by the sea."

The ministry of the word is not entrusted to angels or spirits but to mankind. So the angel directed him to the apostle Peter (a man called and commissioned by Christ to preach the good news to mankind), so he could show him the way of salvation.

Ephesians 1:11 says God works all things according to the counsel of his will. The will of God concerning the ministry of the word was that the apostle Peter would preach the gospel message to the Jews, while Paul would minister to the gentiles.

THE PRAYER OF CORNELIUS

On the contrary, when they saw that I had been entrusted with the gospel to the uncircumcised, just as Peter had been entrusted with the gospel to the circumcised (for he who worked through Peter for his apostolic ministry to the circumcised worked also through me for mine to the Gentiles), and when James and Cephas and John, who seemed to be pillars, perceived the grace that was given to me, they gave the right hand of fellowship to Barnabas and me, that we should go to the Gentiles and they to the circumcised.
(Gal.2:7-9 ESV)

Cornelius was a gentile, and according to the order of things as planned by God, the apostle Paul was the chosen vessel to preach the good news to him. At this time, Paul wasn't ready for the task, because he had just been converted from Judaism to Christianity in the preceding chapter (Acts 9:1-31).

If Cornelius would have had to wait for him (Paul), it would have taken him another fourteen years (Gal.2:1). But his persistent prayer moved God to change the order of things, interrupt Peter's mission to the Jews, and use him for the occasion to minister to Cornelius and his family so they could be saved. The Lord couldn't wait for Paul, who he chose in eternity past for the task, because that would take a longer period of time. So, he used Peter to accomplish the task that Paul would have done, due to the intensity of Cornelius prayer.

Getting the apostle Peter to do this work would take only God because of many things that stood between him and Cornelius. First, the Jewish religion, laws, and customs forbade him (Peter) to enter the house of the gentiles because of their practices and way of life.

UNDERSTANDING the Art of Prayer (Revisited)

The gentiles eat and do things that the Jews were not allowed to do by the law, which made it impossible for both parties to associate.

To the Jews, the gentiles are unclean and uncircumcised, so they must not associate with them. This became a stronghold in the mind of Peter that no matter what you did or said, he wouldn't accept going to Cornelius or entering his home. If he went there, he would have broken the Law of Moses and been seen as unclean by others. He would have been highly criticized by his fellow Jews, and his authority would have been undermined.

God had to step in, orchestrate a situation to break the stronghold in his mind, and suspend the Law of Moses that was against Cornelius by causing Peter to hunger. He then put Peter in a trance before removing the stigma that the Jewish laws and traditions had placed on Cornelius and his whole family. The Holy Spirit had to instruct him to go to Cornelius' house without hesitation before Peter finally went.

About noon the following day as they were on their journey and approaching the city, Peter went up on the roof to pray. He became hungry and wanted something to eat, and while the meal was being prepared, he fell into a trance. He saw heaven opened and something like a large sheet being let down to earth by its four corners. It contained all kinds of four-footed animals, as well as reptiles of the earth and birds of the air. Then a voice told him, "Get up, Peter. Kill and eat." "Surely not, Lord!" Peter replied. "I have never eaten anything impure or unclean." The voice spoke to him a second time, "Do not call anything impure that God has made clean." This happened three times, and immediately the sheet was taken back to heaven.

THE PRAYER OF CORNELIUS

While Peter was wondering about the meaning of the vision, the men sent by Cornelius found out where Simon's house was and stopped at the gate. They called out, asking if Simon who was known as Peter was staying there. While Peter was still thinking about the vision, the Spirit said to him, "Simon, three men are looking for you. So get up and go downstairs. Do not hesitate to go with them, for I have sent them.
(Acts 10:9-20 NIV)

Cornelius' persistent prayer gave him what he could not achieve by any other means. What his citizenship, achievement, contacts, influence, status, success, family, etc. could not give him came by way of prayer.

His persistent prayer moved God, provoked angelic intervention, released divine direction to where his helper was staying, broke the yoke of delay, reduced the time from fourteen years to two days, changed the divine order of things from Paul to Peter, overturned the laws, traditions, and customs that disqualified him and stood on his way. It also destroyed the strongholds in Peter's mind, removed the label and stigma that the Jewish religion placed on Cornelius and his family, attracted the voice of the Spirit, and brought salvation to his entire family.

This is what prayer can do. When everything else fails, resort to prayer, and you will experience the wonder-working power that will turn things around in your life.

So Peter was kept in prison; but earnest prayer for him was made to God by the church. The very night when Herod was about to bring him out, Peter was sleeping between two soldiers, bound with two chains, and sentries before the door were guarding the prison; and behold, an angel of the Lord appeared, and a light shone in the cell; and he struck Peter on the side and woke him, saying, "Get up quickly." And the chains fell off his hands. And the angel said to him, "Dress yourself and put on your sandals." And he did so. And he said to him, "Wrap your mantle around you and follow me."
(Acts 12:5-8 RSV)

CHAPTER 11

PRAYER WORKS

From the little we have learned so far about prayer, I believe you will all agree with me that prayer really works. It works for those who knows the "how-to" and understands the "know-how." The Bible shows us from Genesis to Revelation, how men and women of old used it to move the mighty hand of God, provoke angelic intervention, turn miserable situation around, bring dead situation to life, secure victory and recover lost territories etc.

In this chapter, we shall take a quick look at some incredible things people accomplished in the Bible through prayer, learn from their experiences, and see how best we could use the same prayer to do great things in our time.

Hebrew 13:8, says "Jesus is the same yesterday, today, and forever." God never changes. His promises are yes and amen. What he did yesterday, he can do the same today. The same way he answered the prayers of those in the Bible, he can do the same for us. And if prayers worked for men and women of old, it will work for us. Prayer still works!

PETER'S MIRACULOUS ESCAPE FROM JAIL

Acts 12:1-19 recounts how King Herod persecuted the church in an attempt to destroy it so that he could stay popular with the Jewish leaders who opposed the church and were doing everything within their power to stop it. He arrested some of the leaders of the church and killed James the brother of John with the sword.

When he saw that this pleased the Jews, he proceeded to seize Peter also so he could kill him the same way he killed James, but his evil agenda was intercepted and aborted by the prayer of the church. Having arrested Peter, King Herod put him in prison so he could arrange a public trial for him after the Passover.

The king took extra measures and placed Peter under the guard of four squads of four soldiers each (a total of sixteen soldiers) to make sure he did not escape from custody. Peter and James were both leaders and pillars in the early church (Gal.2:9). It would have been improper for King Herod to bring Peter to trial during such a holy Jewish celebration. But keeping him in custody gave the church an opportunity to pray without ceasing to God for Peter.

It happened that the night before Peter was to be placed on trial, he was sleeping between two soldiers, bound with two chains, and sentries stood guard at the prison gate. Suddenly, an angel of the Lord appeared in the cell. He woke Peter up and said, "Quick, get up!" The chains immediately fell off Peter's wrists. Then the angel said to him, "Put on your clothes and sandals and follow me."

PRAYER WORKS

Peter followed him out of the prison, but he didn't realize that what the angel was doing was really happening; he thought he was seeing a vision. When they had passed the first and second guards, they came to the iron gate leading to the city, and it opened for them by itself. They went through it and started walking down the street, and suddenly the angel left him.

When Peter came to his senses, he said, "Now I know without a doubt that the Lord has sent his angel and rescue me from the hand of Herod and from all that the Jewish people were hoping would happen."

He went to the house of the mother of Mark, where many people had gathered and were praying. He knocked at the door, and a servant named Rhoda came to answer, but when she heard Peter's voice, she recognized it. She was so excited that instead of opening the door, she ran back inside and told everyone, "Peter is standing at the door!"

They could not believe what she was saying. At first, they said she was out of her mind, but when she insisted, they said, "It is his angel!" Meanwhile, Peter continued knocking and when they opened the door, they saw him and were all astonished. He motioned with his hand for them to be quiet, and he described how the Lord had brought him out of the prison.

The miracle was so astounding that they could not believe it. It was beyond what they expected. Everyone knew Herod was going to kill Peter when he arrested him. So they all came together to intercede for him. Their intercession moved the hand of God and deployed his angel in Peter's favor, to rescue him from the evil plan of Herod and the Jewish leaders.

Their continual travailing prayer overturned the plot of the wicked, delivered the apostle Peter from death, and rescued the church from destruction.

The apostle James, whom King Herod killed with the sword, would not have died had the church stood for him in prayer like they did for Peter. Prayer is a great weapon that we can use to protect and preserve whatever God has given us. When the enemies attack, you can use the power of prayer to block and frustrate their evil agenda. Prayer can be used as a protective and preventive weapon.

PROTECTIVE AND PREVENTIVE POWER OF PRAYER

For every action of God, expect a reaction from the enemy. The wicked always plan to counteract or undo whatever God does. John 11:1-44 describes how Lazarus died and was buried, but Jesus came after four days and raised him to life. The news about it spread everywhere and many who saw the miracle put their faith in Jesus.

Sometime later, Jesus came to Bethany, where Lazarus lived, and a dinner was prepared for him. Martha Served and Lazarus was one of those who ate with him. When the people found out that Jesus was there, a large crowd of the Jews came not for Jesus' sake only, but also to see Lazarus, whom he had raised from the dead.

PRAYER WORKS

At the same time, the chief priests made plans to kill Lazarus, because on account of him many of the Jews were going away and believing in Jesus (Jn. 12:1-11). Can you imagine what it would have been like if the wicked had succeeded in killing Lazarus the second time? Sickness attacked and killed him at first, but Jesus came and raised him from the dead. This time, men were plotting to kill him just because people were putting their faith in Christ on account of him.

You must understand that whatever God gives you is a threat to your enemies. The wicked will either try to destroy your miracles or make you lose them by all means. I decree and declare by divine authority that you shall not loss whatever God has given you, in Jesus mighty name. Amen!

God has given us some weapons to safeguard our miracle against any kind of aggression, and prayer is one of them. It is a protective and preventive weapon that can be used to secure, protect, and preserve one's destiny, life, and family.

One of the main reasons a lot of people lose their miracle or testimonies is that they sleep when they ought to watch and protect what they have. Many go to sleep after obtaining their miracles. If Mary and her sister Martha had waited for the wicked to strike before taking action, they would have lost their brother Lazarus the second time.

They were both proactive in safeguarding what God gave them. Martha gave a dinner in honor of Jesus, while Mary sacrificed a very expensive perfume and poured it on Jesus feet and then wiped it with her hair.

UNDERSTANDING the Art of Prayer (Revisited)

Jesus was already in their house before the enemies started plotting on how to destroy their miracle. One of the ways to bring God into your home or situation is prayer, and when God is in your house, he protects and preserves whatever you have.

The Lord Jesus gave a parable in Matthew 13:24-30 about a man who planted good seeds in his field, but while everyone was sleeping, his enemy came and sowed weeds among the wheat and went away.

Another parable he put before them, saying, "The kingdom of heaven may be compared to a man who sowed good seed in his field; but while men were sleeping, his enemy came and sowed weeds among the wheat, and went away. So when the plants came up and bore grain, then the weeds appeared also. And the servants of the householder came and said to him, 'Sir, did you not sow good seed in your field? How then has it weeds?' He said to them, 'An enemy has done this.' The servants said to him, 'Then do you want us to go and gather them?' But he said, 'No; lest in gathering the weeds you root up the wheat along with them. Let both grow together until the harvest; and at harvest time I will tell the reapers, Gather the weeds first and bind them in bundles to be burned, but gather the wheat into my barn.'
(Matt.13:24-30RSV)

When the crop began to grow and produce grain, the weeds also appeared. The owner's servant went to him and said, "Sir, didn't you sow good seed in your field? Where then did the weeds come from?" "An enemy did this," he replied.

To the owner, it was just an enemy who did it. But the passage says it wasn't just an enemy, but the enemy of the man came while everyone was sleeping.

PRAYER WORKS

Whether you believe it or not, we all have enemies, and we all have unguarded hours. The enemies will always come to steal, kill, and destroy at the moment we are not expecting (Jn. 10.10).

The Bible admonishes us in Mark 14:38 to watch and pray in order not to fall into temptation. For our adversary the devil is an opportunist, and he seeks occasion and takes advantage of every chance he finds. Prayer is a sure weapon that you can use to block every demonic onslaught and to overturn the devices of the enemy.

When the Israelites went out of Egypt, the Bible declares that they plundered the Egyptians. That is to say, they came out with abundant wealth (Ex.12:36). Exodus 14:5 says when word reached Pharaoh that the people of Israel had fled, he and his officials changed their minds. "Why have we let the Israelites go from serving us?" they asked. So he prepared his chariot and took six hundred of the best chariots of Egypt, with officers over all of them.

Pharaoh, with all his army, chased after the Israelites to bring them back to bondage after four hundred and thirty years in slavery. It's one thing to get a miracle, but another to keep and maintain it.

This reminds me of a passage in 1 Kings 3:16-28 that talks about two prostitutes living alone in the same house who had babies almost at the same time. Out of negligence, one of them laid on her son, and when she realized he was dead, she got up at the middle of the night and took the other woman's living child. She then put her dead son by the side of the other woman while she was asleep.

When she rose in the morning to nurse her child, she noticed that her son was dead, but as she observed him closely, she saw that the dead child was not her son.

UNDERSTANDING the Art of Prayer (Revisited)

This led to a severe battle between the two of them, but it was too late, because she slept when she should have watched over her son and stopped the other woman from taking him away.

Had she kept watch, the wicked would not have switched or exchanged her living son at midnight. She waited until things fell apart before crying out to the king for help, and had it not been for the wisdom God gave to Solomon, she would never had recovered her stolen child. When we fall asleep spiritually, we give the wicked occasion to advance their demonic agenda. I overturn any demonic exchange in your life, and I command whatever the wicked had tempered with or switched to be reversed, in Jesus name. Amen!

Whenever God blesses us, the wicked come to take it from our hand, because they don't want us to enjoy the blessing. The main reason a lot of people lose their miracle is spiritual slumber. When you don't watch and pray, you give the wicked free access to your life. Prayer is a strong weapon that you can use to protect all that you have and prevent the wicked from infiltrating your home.

When Haman son of Hammedatha, the Agagite, the enemy of the Jews, plotted to annihilate the Jewish people, he approached the King Ahasuerus and said to him, "There is a certain people scattered abroad and dispersed among the people in all the provinces of your kingdom. Their laws are different from those of every other people, and they do not keep the king's laws; it is not in the king's best interest to tolerate them. If it pleases the king, let a decree be issued to destroy them, and I will pay ten thousands talents of silver to the king's administrator for the royal treasury."

PRAYER WORKS

The king took his signet ring from his finger and gave it to Haman. He said to him, "Keep the money and do with the people as you please." Then the royal secretaries were summoned to write in the script of each province and in the language of each people all that Haman instructed them to write to the king's highest officers, the governors and nobles of each province. It was written in the name of King Ahasuerus and sealed with his ring. The edict was to kill, destroy, and annihilate all the Jews (young and old, women, and children), on a single day, and to plunder their goods (Esther 3:8-15).

When Mordecai learned about this edict, he cried out with a loud and bitter cry. He told Hathach, one of the king's eunuchs assigned to attend to Queen Esther, all that had happened to his people, including the amount of money Haman had promised to pay into the royal treasury for the destruction of the Jews. He also gave him a copy of the edict for their destruction to show to Esther and explained the whole thing to her, so that she would go to the king and plead with him for on behalf of her people.

When Hathach reported the words of Mordecai to Esther, she sent him back to Mordecai with the following message, "All the king's servants and the people of the royal provinces know that if a man or woman goes to the king in the inner court without being invited, there is but one law: that they be put to death, except the one to whom the king holds out the golden scepter and spares their lives. The king has not called for me to come to him for thirty days."

Queen Esther knew how important it was for her to plead with the king on behalf of her people for mercy, but there was a law that stood on her way (a death sentence).

UNDERSTANDING the Art of Prayer (Revisited)

Knowing the power of fasting and prayer, she asked all her people to fast and pray three days for her so that the law that killed and destroyed others would not harm her (Esther 4:1-17).

The fasting and prayer of the Jewish people, suspended indefinitely, the force of the law that should have destroyed Esther, so that she could go into the inner court of the king without being sent for, and plead with him on behalf of her people (Esther 5:1-3). Had it not been for the prayer of her people, the law that stood against her would have killed her. The protective and preventive power of prayer blocked the force of the law. I command any evil law working against you and your family to be overturned, in Jesus name. Amen!

When King David heard that his adviser Ahithophel was among the conspirators with Absalom, he was scared, and he prayed that God would turn Ahithopel's counsel to foolishness (2 Sam.15:31). In addition, he sent his friend Hushai the Arkite to the palace to help him frustrate Ahithophel's advice to Absalom. The reason for this is that Ahithophel's advice was as though one inquired of the Lord.

The man knew David's strength and weakness — only he knew the amount of soldier needed to take King David down in warfare. 2 Samuel 17:1 says that he asked Absalom for twelve thousand chosen men to pursue David and strike him down while he was still weak and weary, for he knew how skillful and fierce David and his men were in the battlefield.

The Bible declares that God frustrated the good advice of Ahithophel in order to bring disaster on Absalom, and when he saw that his counsel was not accepted, he went home, put his house in order and hanged himself (2 Sam.17:14 and 23). Had it not been for the prayer of David, he would have been destroyed through the advice Ahithophel gave to Absalom against him. By my prayer, let every evil counsel and decision taken against you and your family be turned to foolishness, in the name of Jesus. Amen!

ROLE OF PRAYER IN DISCOVERING YOUR DIVINE PURPOSE

Your divine purpose is the main reason God created you. It is your primary assignment on earth. Nothing else matters more to God than his purpose for a thing, and he will do anything to make it stand. Proverbs 19:21 says many are the plans in a man's heart, but it is the purpose of the Lord that will stand.

Discovering one's divine purpose is essential to living a fulfilled life. God is spirit, and his will is spiritually discerned. 1 Corinthians 2:14 declares that a natural person cannot receive the things of the spirit because they sound foolish to him, for he is not able to understand or discern them. To grasp spiritual things, one has to be spiritually alert. This is where prayer comes in, because it raises your spiritual antennae so you can apprehend and decode spiritual things.

Jeremiah 1:4-10 informs us how Jeremiah had a divine encounter that changed the course of his life from being a priest to an outstanding prophet.

UNDERSTANDING the Art of Prayer (Revisited)

He was born a priest, educated and raised to be the best priest of his time. He was probably taught the different utensils in the temple and how to use them.

These are the words of Jeremiah son of Hilkiah, one of the priests from the town of Anathoth in the land of Benjamin. The Lord first gave messages to Jeremiah during the thirteenth year of the reign of Josiah son of Amon, king of Judah. The Lord's messages continued throughout the reign of King Jehoiakim, Josiah's son, until the eleventh year of the reign of King Zedekiah, another of Josiah's sons. In August of that eleventh year the people of Jerusalem were taken away as captives. The Lord gave me this message: "I knew you before I formed you in your mother's womb. Before you were born I set you apart and appointed you as my prophet to the nations." "O Sovereign Lord," I said, "I can't speak for you! I'm too young!" The Lord replied, "Don't say, 'I'm too young,' for you must go wherever I send you and say whatever I tell you. And don't be afraid of the people, for I will be with you and will protect you. I, the Lord, have spoken!" Then the Lord reached out and touched my mouth and said, "Look, I have put my words in your mouth! Today I appoint you to stand up against nations and kingdoms. Some you must uproot and tear down, destroy and overthrow. Others you must build up and plant."
(Jer.1:1-10 NLT)

As a young priest born in the city of priests, Jeremiah would have been taught the lifestyle of the priests and been encouraged to eat, dress, speak, walk, and live like a priest. His whole life, purpose, vision, dream, education, and so on were fashioned in light of the priestly ministry because of his birth, community, education, daily activities, family traditions, and practices.

PRAYER WORKS

But in the mind of God, Jeremiah was a prophet, not a priest, even though his whole life perfectly fits to the priestly ministry.

When you look at the prophetic and priestly ministries, the difference is so huge that none could ever imagine that a person like Jeremiah was a prophet clothed in a priestly garment. The traditions and practices of the prophetic ministry are so different from that of the priestly ministry that Jeremiah could never see himself as a prophet.

On the outside, he was a priest in the making, but on the inside, he was an ordained major prophet. It took God's intervention to uncover Jeremiah's true purpose and identity. When God stepped in, he interrupted everything, opening Jeremiah's eyes to his divine purpose and giving him specific direction that would help him fulfill his destiny.

The Lord said to him, "Before I formed you in the womb I knew you, and before you were born I consecrated you; I appointed you a prophet to the nations." This means that Jeremiah was formed in view of what he was coming to accomplish on earth, but the environment into which he was born shifted his focus and gave him a new purpose to serve, which was different from his original assignment.

Nothing in the world exists without a purpose, and it is the purpose of a thing that determines its making. Before anything is ever made, the purpose is first established, so that when it is built, it can deliver the intended result.

The Lord has a purpose for everything he does, and his purpose takes precedence over everything else.

UNDERSTANDING the Art of Prayer (Revisited)

Proverbs 19:21 says many are the plans in a man's heart, but it is the purpose of God that will stand. In Isaiah 14:24, the Lord swore that as he planned, so it would be, and as he purposed, so it will happen. Heaven and earth may pass away, but God's eternal purpose concerning a thing stands forever.

When God sees you are marking time, he orchestrates things to align you with your divine purpose, just as he did for Jeremiah to turn him from his own way as priest to his divine purpose — a prophet. May you be in perfect alignment with your divine purpose, in Jesus name. Amen

No one in Jeremiah's house had ever been a prophet, and by way of things, he was raised to be the best prophet of his time until God stepped in and unfolded his original intent, which was established before Jeremiah was conceived in the womb.

At first Jeremiah struggled with it and had difficulty accepting it because it was contrary to what he believed he was born to do. He made a lot of excuses to avoid the purpose and to stick to what he knew how to do best. God had to call him out of what culture and traditions had programmed him to do for a living and then commission him to do what he was born to do. The passage below shows the struggle and difficulty Jeremiah had before accepting his divine purpose (the main reason he was born).

Now the word of the Lord came to me saying, "Before I formed you in the womb I knew you, and before you were born I consecrated you; I appointed you a prophet to the nations." Then I said, "Ah, Lord God! Behold, I do not know how to speak, for I am only a youth." But the Lord said to me, "Do not say, 'I am only a youth'; for to all to whom I send you you shall go,

and whatever I command you you shall speak. Be not afraid of them, for I am with you to deliver you, says the Lord." Then the Lord put forth his hand and touched my mouth; and the Lord said to me, "Behold, I have put my words in your mouth. See, I have set you this day over nations and over kingdoms, to pluck up and to break down, to destroy and to overthrow, to build and to plant."
(Jer. 1:4-10 RSV)

Luke 1:39-44 also relates how Mary went to the hill country of Judea to meet her relative Elizabeth, after the angel Gabriel spoke to her that she (Mary) would conceive and give birth to a son, whom she was to name Jesus. She went there because the angel told her that Elizabeth, who was barren, had finally conceived in her old age, and that she was already in her sixth month.

When Mary arrived at Zechariah's home to confirm what the angel told her, she greeted Elizabeth. As soon as Elizabeth heard Mary's voice, her six month old baby leaped for joy in her womb because he felt the presence of Jesus. He knew immediately that the main reason he was coming to the earth was to make ready a people for the Lord Jesus. He was so clear about his primary assignment that he didn't need anyone to introduce Jesus to him. Mary's voice alone was enough to connect him to his primary assignment.

Thirty years later, John the Baptist said about Jesus that he would not have known him, except that the Father who sent him to baptize gave him a sign that enabled him to identify Jesus from among those who came to be baptized. How is it that when he was six months old in the womb, he recognized Jesus as soon as he heard Mary's voice, but thirty years after he was born, he couldn't recognize him anymore?

UNDERSTANDING the Art of Prayer (Revisited)

The next day John saw Jesus coming toward him and said, "Look, the Lamb of God, who takes away the sin of the world! This is the one I meant when I said, 'A man who comes after me has surpassed me because he was before me.' I myself did not know him, but the reason I came baptizing with water was that he might be revealed to Israel." Then John gave this testimony: "I saw the Spirit come down from heaven as a dove and remain on him. I would not have known him, except that the one who sent me to baptize with water told me, 'The man on whom you see the Spirit come down and remain is he who will baptize with the Holy Spirit.' I have seen and I testify that this is the Son of God."
(Jn.1:29-34 NIV)

This happened to John because of the condition of the human spirit and body. The human spirit loses connection with heavenly things once on earth because of the sin of Adam that makes it dormant on earth. Since the human body was taken from the dust of the earth, according to scripture (Gen.3:19), it gravitates toward worldly things.

Had God not given John a sign about Jesus, he would not have recognized him. He had to search and discover his purpose because a lot of things clouded his view and hid it from him. Without the sign God gave him, he wouldn't have discovered his purpose. There are many signs or indicators that could help you discover your divine purpose in life, and prayer is one of them.

The role of prayer in discovering ones divine purpose is so important that it cannot be overlooked. Prayer provokes divine intervention and direction, and it births and enforces God's kingdom and divine will on earth.

PRAYER WORKS

When you pray, you give God authorization to interfere with your affairs so he can change your path and direct you into his purpose for your life. Prayer raises your spiritual antennae and increases your ability to apprehend and comprehend spiritual things.

The human mind can't receive the things of the spirit, because they are spiritually discerned. It takes the inner work of the Holy Spirit for a person to understand the things of the spirit. God's purpose is spiritual and eternal. Unless the Holy Spirit helps us, we cannot understand it. The Holy Spirit won't work in us without our cooperation, and one of the ways we collaborate with him is through prayer. When we pray, the Lord uses it to direct our paths into his plan and purpose for our lives.

In the parable of the talents, Jesus talks about a man who called his servants and entrusted his property to them. To one he gave five talents, to another two talents, and to the last one talent — to every man according to his ability.

Luke's version of the same story says the master instructed them to put their talents to work and make profit with them (Lk.19:13). This was the main reason he gave them the talents. But the talents were given to them according to their individual abilities, which implies that your natural abilities determine the nature of gifts you have. However, your gifts and divine purpose are directly related. If you identify your strength zone, you will discover your gifts. And your gift is a pointer to your divine assignment. Unless you discover your gift and activate it, you cannot fully fulfill your purpose.

UNDERSTANDING the Art of Prayer (Revisited)

Your natural ability is your strength zone, your area of excellence and effectiveness. The question you should ask yourself is: What one thing could I do, and do it so well that I could be the best at it in the whole world? What are you naturally inclined to? What are you passionate about? What do you do easily and freely that other people find difficult and somewhat impossible? What is your area of excellence? What energizes you and could keep you awake all night? What is that thing that gives you joy and that you could willingly do without being paid for it (no financial reward)? That is the area of effectiveness where your gifts are hidden.

Your gift is that special skill or talent that makes you unique. It sets you apart from the pack and makes you act differently. When you prayerfully search your strength zone, you will uncover the hidden talents God gave you to fulfill your divine purpose. Once you discover the gift, activate or put it to work, and then set goals that you could accomplish using the unique talent.

When the purpose you are serving, the talents you have, and your natural abilities are perfectly in alignment, you will lead a happy and fulfilled life, because your natural abilities determine the kind of gifts you have, while the gifts reflect the purpose you were born to serve. Having these three in perfect alignment gives you a sense of direction, motivation, focus, and strength, and makes you purposeful in life.

Going back to the story of the talents, the passage shows how the one who received five talents multiplied it to ten, and the one with two multiplied his to four, but the one to whom the master gave one talent dug a hole in the ground and hid it.

PRAYER WORKS

After some time, the master returned and called them to give an account of how they had used the talents he gave them. Those who put their talents to work, multiplied them, and made profit with them for their master were greatly rewarded.

So he who had received five talents came and brought five other talents, saying, "Lord, you delivered to me five talents; look, I have gained five more talents besides them.'" His lord said to him, "'Well done, good and faithful servant; you were faithful over a few things, I will make you ruler over many things. Enter into the joy of your lord." He also who had received two talents came and said, "Lord, you delivered to me two talents; look, I have gained two more talents besides them." His lord said to him, "Well done, good and faithful servant; you have been faithful over a few things, I will make you ruler over many things. Enter into the joy of your lord." Then he who had received the one talent came and said, "Lord, I knew you to be a hard man, reaping where you have not sown, and gathering where you have not scattered seed. And I was afraid, and went and hid your talent in the ground. Look, there you have what is yours." But his lord answered and said to him, "You wicked and lazy servant, you knew that I reap where I have not sown, and gather where I have not scattered seed. So you ought to have deposited my money with the bankers, and at my coming I would have received back my own with interest. So take the talent from him, and give it to him who has ten talents. For to everyone who has, more will be given, and he will have abundance; but from him who does not have, even what he has will be taken away. And cast the unprofitable servant into the outer darkness. There will be weeping and gnashing of teeth."
(Matt.25:20-30 NKJV)

Just as the passage clearly reveals, the servant that buried his talent lost it all in the end. His master called him a worthless servant and commanded the others to throw him into the outer darkness, where there will be weeping and gnashing of teeth. But the one who already had ten was given more because he put the five he received to work and multiplied them.

The role of prayer in all of these is that it raises your spiritual antennae and makes you very sensitive to spiritual things so that you can easily identify your gift, activate it, discover your purpose, and use the gift to fulfill it. Prayer helps you to stay on track and puts you on guard against the plan of the wicked.

ROLE OF PRAYER IN BIRTHING YOUR PROPHETIC DESTINY

The Israelites lived in Egypt for a long time, and during that period, it appeared as if the promise God made to their ancestors regarding the land of Canaan, which he swore to give them, was forgotten and abandoned, because things were going well for every one of them in Egypt. They prospered and greatly multiplied until the day everything suddenly turned against them and life became very uncomfortable for them all.

The Scripture tells us that a new king, who did not regard Joseph or the things he did for Egypt, came to power. He said to his people that the Israelites had outnumbered them and that if they did not make a plan to stop the people from becoming more numerous, they would join the enemies of Egypt in battle and fight against the Egyptians if war broke out, and then they would leave the country (Ex.1:6-10).

PRAYER WORKS

For this reason, the Egyptians devised strategies that they used to make the Israelites their slaves, and they set taskmasters over them to oppress and afflict them with heavy burdens. They forced the people of Israel to build Pithom and Rameses as store cities for Pharaoh. In addition, Pharaoh gave order to his people to throw every newborn Hebrew boy into the Nile, but to let the girls live. This made the life of the Israelites very unpleasant and frustrating in Egypt.

As the affliction continued, things went from bad to worse for the people of God, until they couldn't stand the oppression anymore. So, they began to groan in their slavery and cried out to the Lord for help because of their affliction. Exodus 2:23-25 declares that their cry for rescue from slavery went up to God and the Lord heard their groaning, so he remembered his covenant with Abraham, Isaac, and Jacob. The long forgotten and neglected promise of God concerning their destiny came back to life when they started crying out to God in prayer.

Exodus 3:1-10 shows us how God moved to Median after the cry and groaning of his people in Egypt went up to him in heaven in order to search for Moses, the man he appointed to bring the Israelites out of bondage. At this time, Moses was busy tending the flock of Jethro his father in-law in a foreign land, while the people he was destined to liberate from bondage were suffering in Egypt. All of his attention was centered on his wife and the work he was doing in Midian until God appeared on the scene.

The passage says that the angel of the Lord appeared to him (Moses) in flames of fire from the middle of a bush as he walked by with his flock to the wilderness.

He saw that though the bush was on fire, it wasn't consumed. The sight caught his attention, and he decided he would go over to see why the bush was not burned up.

When the Lord saw that he turned to see what was happening to the tree, God called to him from within the bush, "Moses, Moses." And he answered, "Here I am." God presented himself to Moses and explained the reason he had come to him.

He said, "I have surely seen the affliction of my people who are in Egypt and have heard their cry because of their taskmasters. I know their sufferings, and I have come down to deliver them out of the hand of the Egyptians and to bring them up out of that land to a good and broad land, a land flowing with milk and honey, to the place of the Canaanites, the Hittites, the Amorites, the Perizzites, the Hivites, and the Jebusites. And now, behold, the cry of the people of Israel has come to me, and I have also seen the oppression with which the Egyptians oppress them. Come, I will send you to Pharaoh that you may bring my people, the children of Israel, out of Egypt."

Had the people not cried out to God in prayer, he would not have gone out to Midian in search for Moses, whom he had ordained to bring them out of bondage to the land he swore to their ancestors. Their prayer activated the power of the covenant God made with father Abraham, and moved the Lord to intervene in their situation. The intervention of God obliged the Egyptians to force the Israelites out of Egypt so they could go to Canaan land and fulfill their divine assignment (Ex.12:31-33).

PRAYER WORKS

Just as it was in old times, prayer still plays an important role in birthing one's prophetic destiny. Even Jesus, our Lord and Savior, had to pray earnestly to birth his prophetic destiny. Scripture shows how he struggled between his will and the predetermined will of the Godhead concerning him during his earthly ministry.

Matthew 26:36-44 describes how he persistently prayed that the Father would take the cup from him. He fell down three consecutive times in prayer, saying the same thing — that the Father would take the cup from him. To let go of his own will and superimpose the counsel of the Father over his life, the Bible says an angel came from heaven to strengthen him. And being in agony, he prayed earnestly until his sweat fell to the ground like great drops of blood to birth his prophetic destiny and save humanity from eternal condemnation (Lk.22:39-46). Prayer has always work, and it will continue to work for those who knows the "how-to" and understands the "know-how."

About eight days after Jesus said this, he took Peter, John and James with him and went up onto a mountain to pray. As he was praying, the appearance of his face changed, and his clothes became as bright as a flash of lightning. Two men, Moses and Elijah, appeared in glorious splendor, talking with Jesus. They spoke about his departure, which he was about to bring to fulfillment at Jerusalem.
(Lk. 9:28-31 NIV)

IMPORTANT ABBREVIATIONS

Gen. .... Genesis
Ex. .... Exodus
Lev. .... Leviticus
Num. .... Numbers
Deut. .... Deuteronomy
Josh. .... Joshua
Judg. .... Judges
1Sa. 1Samuel
2Sa. 2Samuel
1Ki. 1Kings
2Ki. .... 2 Kings
1Ch. 1Chronicles
2Ch. 2Chronicles
Neh. .... Nehemiah
Esth. .... Esther
Ps. .... Psalms
Pr. .... Proverbs
Ecc. .... Ecclesiastics
SoS. .... Song of Songs
Is. .... Isaiah
Jer. .... Jeremiah
Lam. .... Lamentations
Ezek. .... Ezekiel
Dan. .... Daniel
Hos. .... Hosea
Jon. .... Jonah
Mic. .... Micah
Nah. .... Nahum
Hab. .... Habakkuk
Zeph. .... Zephaniah
Hag. .... Haggai
Zec. .... Zechariah

Matt.	Matthew
Mk.	Mark
Lk.	Luke
Jn.	John
Rom.	Romans
1Co.	1Corinthians
2Co.	2Corinthians
Gal.	Galatians
Eph.	Ephesians
Phi.	Philippians
Col.	Colossians
1Thes.	1Thessalonians
2Thes.	2Thessalonians
1Tim.	1Timothy
2Tim.	2Timothy
Heb.	Hebrews
Jas.	James
1Pet.	1Peter
2Pet.	2Peter
1Jn.	1John
2Jn.	2John
3Jn.	3John
Rev.	Revelation

PRAYER OF SALVATION

The gospel message also known as the word of faith, belief and open confession play distinct roles in the salvation process, according to Romans10:8-10. The word of faith produces the faith we need to please God and be at peace with him (Heb.11:6), believing that God raised Jesus from death causes him to impute his righteousness that is by faith to us (Rom.4:22-25). Confessing the lordship of Jesus makes God to infuse our spirit with his eternal life for rebirth.

Salvation does not come by merely verbalizing the *Sinner's Prayer* without faith in Christ atoning sacrifice that comes from hearing the gospel message, repentance from dead works, and open confession of Jesus Christ as Lord and Savior.

1. Believe in your heart that Christ is the Son of the living God.
2. Believe he died on the cross for your sins and iniquities.
3. Believe that God raised him from the dead after three days for your justification.
4. Believe he is at the right hand of the Father in heaven interceding for you.
5. Believe that only Christ has the legitimate right to give eternal life to humans.
6. Ask him to forgive your sins and wash you by his blood.
7. Openly declare him lord of your life from the depth of your heart.
8. Invite him to come and dwell in you.
9. Ask him to write your name in the book of life.

And this is the testimony: God has given us eternal life, and this life is in his Son. He who has the Son has life; he who does not have the Son of God does not have life. I write these things to you who believe in the name of the Son of God so that you may know that you have eternal life.
(1 Jn. 5:11-14 NIV)

If you confess with your mouth the Lord Jesus and believe in your heart that God has raised Him from the dead, you will be saved. For with the heart one believes unto righteousness, and with the mouth confession is made unto salvation.
(Rom.10:9-10 NKJV)

Salvation is found in no one else, for there is no other name under heaven given to men by which we must be saved.
(Acts 4:12 NIV)

If we confess our sins, He is faithful and righteous to forgive us our sins and to cleanse us from all unrighteousness.
(1Jn.1:9-10 HCSB)

Once you finish reading the above portion of scriptures, you can make the following confession with me from the depth of your heart. Believe it as you speak, and you shall be saved in Jesus name.

Dear Jesus,

I believe that you died on the cross for my sins, and rose on the third day for my justification. You took away my sins, iniquities, infirmities and blotted out the handwriting of ordinances that were against me by your blood. You were bruised for my transgressions, and became a curse for me in order to redeem my soul from death.

I beseech you Lord to come into my life today, and make my heart your dwelling place. I confess you now as my Lord and Savior. Write my name in the book of life, and make me a new person. Thank you Lord Jesus for saving me. Amen

Congratulation!

And the Lord restored Job's losses when he prayed for his friends. Indeed the Lord gave Job twice as much as he had before. Then all his brothers, all his sisters, and all those who had been his acquaintances before, came to him and ate food with him in his house; and they consoled him and comforted him for all the adversity that the Lord had brought upon him. Each one gave him a piece of silver and each a ring of gold.

(Job 42:10-11 NKJV)

Follow me on  Caesar Benedo
Email.cfnministries@gmail.com

Dépot Légal N° 9604 du 07 / 09 / 2017
Bibliothèque National Du Bénin, 3ème Trimestre

www.ingramcontent.com/pod-product-compliance
Lightning Source LLC
Chambersburg PA
CBHW061646040426
42446CB00010B/1599